A JOURNEY THROUGH
OZ

Carmine,

Good luck
with the Ducla!
(see preface)

Chris Jone

A JOURNEY THROUGH
OZ

THE BUSINESS LEADERS' ROAD MAP TO TRACKING INFORMATION TECHNOLOGY ASSETS

FOURTH EDITION

BY
CHRIS JESSE

KENDALL/HUNT PUBLISHING COMPANY
4050 Westmark Drive   Dubuque, Iowa 52002
(800) 228-0810

Published by
Kendall/Hunt Publishing Company
Dubuque, Iowa
1-800-228-0810

The publishers have given permission to quote from the following
copyrighted works. From *MAN FOR HIMSELF* by Erich Fromm,
Copyright 1947 by Erich Fromm. Reprinted by permission of
Henry Holt & Co., Inc. From *The Lion of Boaz-Jachin*, by Russell
Hoban, Reprinted by permission of Jonathan Cape Publishers,
Hoban/30.10.96.

Cover and text design: John Nedwidek, emdesign
Additional text and chart design: Kathrine Kuo
Copy Editor: Bonnie Tilson

Library of Congress Catalog Card Number: 99-62223

ISBN 0-7872-5991-8

Printed in the United States of America

10 9 8 7 6 5 4 3 2 1

This book is dedicated to Chuck Root, who has shown all who have worked with him how integrity, loyalty, and openness are essential business practices.

THE DISTRIBUTED ENTERPRISE

It was difficult to ascertain the path to my destination, as I was uncertain of my current location. Given this uncertainty, each direction held the promise of both glory and disaster.

• CONTENTS •

CONTENTS

PREFACE

Information technology is a duck. In itself, a duck is a net consumer of resources; it must be contained, requires constant care, becomes less valuable with age, leaves a mess wherever it treads, and is counterproductive until converted into practical application. Caring for ducks requires partners, those who grow the grain, mill the feed, and make the fence wire. Ducks have a mind of their own. They are oblivious to their purpose, and require proactive management if they are to effect a positive result.

Why, in a book about tracking distributed information technology (IT) assets, do I begin with a discussion of ducks? Because as I look at us, those who consume and implement technology, I see that we have become a group of duck aficionados. We have become focused on making faster ducks—whose meat tastes no better, whiter ducks—whose feathers are no softer, bigger ducks—with eggs no larger, and smarter ducks—whose intellect does nothing but make them more difficult to manage.

If technology is to be fully leveraged and is to take its rightful place as a critical thread within the fabric of an organization, we must become duck farmers. This requires that we change our focus from the duck to those consuming the duck, to those supporting our efforts to produce the duck, and to the management of the duck. If we are successful in becoming "duck farmers," our suppliers will become partners, we will assume the mission of the user, and technology will be measured on the rule of mission efficiency.

Becoming a duck farmer requires more than desire and a mission statement; it requires a whole new mind-set. For example, when considering a new implementation of technology for an order entry system, what are the first questions that come to mind? Those focused on the duck find questions such as: What platform and operating system will we use? What is the best way to connect the system? And, what are my resources? While those with a farmer mentality are asking: How much does it cost my users each day they use the old system? Can I modify what is already installed and effect the same results? And, what partners might give me the best ideas?

Because all of this may at first blush seem like esoteric nonsense, I wrote this book around the implementation of a single facet of the "farmer mentality" concept. I regret that I can only address one implementation of this new mind-set. Similar benefits can be found in vendor relations, time-cycle management, user partnering, and many other areas.

Here then is a book written within a broader concept—successfully implemented technology is a single integrated thread within the fabric of the business enterprise. This book—a dramatic and practical example of making the concept a reality.

ACKNOWLEDGMENTS

If you want to know who is truly responsible for any benefit you receive in reading this text, take a moment to skim the names included in the following expression of gratitude.

First, I thank God for all the blessings granted me in allowing this book to be written and published. Primary among those blessings are the scores of individuals who directly and indirectly participated in the intellectual content and creation of this manuscript. As all of these names are too numerous to list, I am forced to thank some contributors as a group. So my first "thank you" goes out to all of those who shared their experiences and trials with me over the past six years. It was their steady progress in managing a base of distributed information technology assets that is the basis for this text. Ladies and gentlemen, your success continues, thank you!

There are also those who offered and sometimes forced their support on me so I might not procrastinate this book out of existence. Thank you Nancy Dunn, Steve Kuekes, Teresa Poppen, and Chuck Root. Without your encouragement and abuse this book would not exist.

My two biggest critics deserve no less thanks as they battled me day after day convincing me that sentences need both a subject and predicate. So thank you Allison David and Tracey Minnich for your relentless editing expertise. I cannot count the number of times you, along with Jim Reece, rescued me from foolishness.

A special thanks to Jae Cody who read this book a dozen times in an effort to give it life and a consistent voice. If this document has a heart, you will find it in rhythm with Jae's pulse.

Finally, I would like to thank my family. Thank you Mandy, Mary, and Rachel, my daughters, and Kay, my mother, for allowing me to use your life experiences as part of this story. Thank you Jennie and Laverne, my dogs, for writing is the loneliest of jobs and you were always there to share the frequent verbal abuse I launched at my word processor. And thank you Judi, my bride, for you are inseparable from any good that comes from me.

So there you have it. The above are those responsible for any merit found in this document. As for the balance, that credit belongs to me, for in spite of my editors' and critics' best efforts, I stand solely responsible for its faults.

INTRODUCTION

Those of you who have seen the movie *The Wizard of Oz* no doubt recognize the title of this book. For those of you who missed the movie, let me briefly set the stage. Dorothy, a young teenager, is swept away by a tornado from the black-and-white world of a Kansas farm to the Technicolor world of the Land of Oz. She looks around and sees colors, landscape, and beings that are beyond her imagination, not to mention her experience, and dryly exclaims to her dog, "Gee, Toto, we're not in Kansas anymore." And so, with this same feeling, I began my precarious journey into the world of managing distributed information technology (IT) resources.

This journey, like Dorothy's, was quite unintentional. As chief executive officer of a software development company, I set out six years ago to deliver a superior electronic software distribution solution. This product, in theory, allowed organizations to electronically distribute new versions of software to distributed desktops and servers (i.e., the distributed enterprise) in an unattended fashion. Thanks to the efforts of some supremely talented individuals, this endeavor succeeded in that several hundred Fortune 500-sized organizations use this product for its intended purpose. This book, however, is not about the success of this product—or for that matter, any product. This book is about the bumps that hundreds of business managers and IT professionals, including myself, encountered as we attempted to embrace an IT enterprise that was geographically dispersed, underfunded, overcommitted, and managed by an anarchy of end users whose vision of the enterprise stopped at their own desktops.

In reality, this book was conceived the first time I asked a very competent Fortune 500 chief information officer, "So what does your distributed enterprise look like?" His answer—and the collective answer I would hear hundreds of times over the next six years—was, "Well, plus or minus 30 percent, I don't have a clue."

His answer did not reflect a lack of competence, but rather the recognition that the enterprise had evolved from both the top down and the bottom up, via local projects and corporate projects, and with a liberal number of end-user authorized and unauthorized changes to a corporate standard that is unenforced by those demanding perfection. Here is the confusing landscape of our electronic Oz.

Yet within this confusion there were those who refused to wander aimlessly. Admittedly, their compass was no better than the rest, but they kept an accurate map of where they had been and were kind enough to share the location of the mile markers they established as part of their journey through the world of managing distributed IT assets. This book is a summary of those mile markers. They allow us to establish our relative position in the journey of managing our distributed IT assets, and they guide us in the general direction of the next known point in our journey.

Two final thoughts. First, if you are looking for an overly serious, statistically based, analytical study of IT asset management, then this book will make a nice coaster for your coffee mug. If on the other hand, you are looking for a dozen or two practical necessities for effectively managing and tracking your distributed IT asset base, then you will have to find another place for your mug. And second, although believing IT asset tracking is critical to the survival of most organizations, I do not rank the topic up there with world hunger or political freedom. Accordingly, I have kept the tone of the book on the light side. This tone is in no way meant to demean the wisdom and experience that has been entrusted to me; it is merely my attempt to construct this book as a conversation between two friends.

Best of luck in Oz...

A JOURNEY THROUGH
OZ

CHAPTER 1
SIMPLE
PROACTIVE MANAGEMENT

Me: *(Saying good-bye to my daughter, as I dropped her off at college at the outset of her freshman year)* I feel like I should say something profound.

Amanda (my daughter): This is pretty confusing; I could use "profound" right now.

Me: The best advice I can give you in your new journey is for you to aspire to simple things, for simplicity and greatness are frequent companions. When you find yourself following a path of increasing complexity, stop!—for you are headed toward diminishing returns.

Amanda: Just as simple as getting good grades, right?

Me: Oh no, good grades are complex. They depend on so many factors: the course material, the professor, your aptitude, and study materials. There's nothing simple about good grades.

Amanda: Then what is simple?

Me: The principles in the Bible, the Spartan's stand at Thermopylae, the calling heard by Martin Luther, and the building of the Hoover Dam—at the heart of each of these is simplicity.

Amanda: You mean focused conviction. How about a commitment to do the very best I can?

Me: You see how simple it is? Amanda, I believe you shall touch greatness.

Amanda excelled in college. She graduated a year early with a double major in English and Spanish. She would tell you the trick to her success was simple: just do the best you can on every homework assignment, every paper, every quiz, every test, and in every class session. Of course she would also add that simple does not necessarily mean easy.

Amanda's learned trick is something that we, in the pursuit of excellence within our organizations, often forget. The greatest progress is made via commitment to simple understandings. I include this bit of philosophy at the beginning of this book as I fear that in my zeal to express the power of managing distributed information technology (IT) resources, I will shroud the topic in complexity. There is nothing complex about the underlying principle of this book. If an organization is going to succeed and survive in the competitive global economy, it must proactively manage its distributed IT resources.

This theorem can be expressed in the form of an equation:

GIVEN
employees = product, creativity, and survival

THEREFORE
employees = our most valued asset

GIVEN
employee productivity = access to a stable base of
distributed IT assets

THEREFORE
proactive management of distributed IT assets = employee
productivity and survival of the organization

This relationship between an employee and technology is of increasing interest to successful management teams. Employees and their desktops are now being viewed as a single unit of productivity (i.e., knowledge unit) as both the employee and the desktop are ineffective without the other. The management of these resources around the knowledge unit concept is simple, yet it offers an extraordinary opportunity to those who focus on its potential.

Forward-thinking industry leaders, including chief information officers (CIOs), chief financial officers (CFOs), purchasing executives, senior general managers, and security and legal professionals, are aggressively pursuing the productivity gains that can be realized via the processes outlined in this book. These gains are expressed in many terms, including improved employee productivity, cost savings, asset leveraging, and expense deferrals; but ultimately, these gains track back to how much additional product we can generate per employee asset. In corporate terms, this is translated into cents per share, return on assets, return on investment, or a host of other measurements. In the end, it is simply the victorious global competitor looking at the vanquished, saying, "My guy can make more than your guy."

What kind of productivity gains can you expect to attain by proactively managing your distributed client/server enterprise assets? To answer this you must estimate how much time average end users spend fighting with the technology on their desktops. How many hours per week is the same average user distracted by the appeal of the Internet's World Wide Web? How much employee productivity is siphoned off by counterproductive upgrades, overpayment to hardware and software suppliers, and theft? The calculation of improved productivity is certainly organization dependent; but responses from knowledgeable executives typically range from 5 to 25 percent.

And so we return to the concept of simplicity. Organizations regularly implement elaborate and complex schemes in an effort to improve the bottom line (e.g., productivity enhancement programs that often net improvement by only tenths of a percentage point). Examples of such activity include whole classes of assets being enveloped in a convoluted lease program to marginally improve financial reports, companies purchasing their own satellite links in an effort to shave a few points off their communications expense, and elaborate self-insurance programs being implemented to modestly reduce the cost of employee benefits. These complex schemes do yield results. However, greater results can be obtained from this simple concept: We need to know what distributed IT assets we have, and we need to proactively manage those assets.

Here, in this simple concept, is the opportunity to realize huge efficiencies. But as Amanda would tell you, simple is not always easy. Putting a man on the moon was driven by man's simple desire to touch the soil of another world. The insurmountable, tedious, complex, and daunting details of this effort were conquered only when viewed through the optics of the dream.

Fortunately, the successful implementation of a solution that allows you to track distributed assets is not a complex task. Such a system (i.e., an asset tracking solution) gives you an understanding of what your assets look like today, as well as the speed and direction of their change. If this book attains its stated purpose, it will provide managers of various disciplines with a blueprint of a solution that delivers the benefits of effective enterprise asset tracking. There will, however, still be challenges along the way, as those responsible for the mission deal with gross World Wide Web abuse, unauthorized software, missing equipment, and disgruntled vendors who have been denied undeserved margins. These challenges and more await those who proactively manage their distributed IT assets. Awaiting too, however, are the disproportionate rewards of embracing the simplicity of productivity.

Here, in these pages, is your map of Oz. The Wizard can be found in the Emerald City…the Yellow Brick Road in chapters 2 through 14. Enjoy the journey.

CHAPTER 2

• BORING BUT NECESSARY •

CONCEPTS AND TERMS

Publisher: You wrote a book on what?

Me: Managing distributed information technology (IT) resources.

Publisher: The what?

Me: You know, a vast network of clients and servers.

Publisher: Who's going to read this book?

Me: People whose professional lives depend on this fragile network of resources.

Publisher: Sorry, we're only going with material that has sex, violence, or the World Wide Web as a theme.

Me: Well, I might be able to work the Web in...

Publisher: Juice it up and shoot me a copy.

As the above conversation highlights, there is no public outcry for a book on managing distributed IT resources. And the reason is simple—most managers have not been exposed to the broad benefits of proactively managing the distributed enterprise. However, once the benefits are understood, even the most detached manager discovers a curiosity for the topic.

It is at this point that the primary obstacle in generating interest is encountered: How do you entertain a spirited dialog on a topic without a common understanding, and how do you gain a common understanding without making an investment in learning the language (terms) of the studied topic? The remainder of this chapter is devoted to establishing a common vocabulary of terms and an understanding of the audience that will benefit from acquiring this knowledge. So then, this is the requisite dry chapter, aptly named "Boring But Necessary." But stick with it, for although it may be boring, it will return big dividends as you move through the more stimulating chapters.

AUDIENCE

As the business benefits of better managing distributed IT assets far outweigh the technical benefits, this book is written at a high level, focusing on business operations. With the exception of chapter 13, all chapters use a minimum of technical jargon and the management of distributed IT assets is approached from a business perspective. Even with this business emphasis, you will find that a high-level discussion of technological concepts is frequently part of a topic. This is necessary because often the specific application of a technology is directly responsible for the associated business benefits. It would be an injustice to you not to tie the two together. Even with the aforementioned confession, this book primarily targets senior managers and executives of large organizations across all industries who are concerned with overall IT resource productivity and utilization. In particular, top executives in the areas of information technology, purchasing, finance, legal, operations, help desk, corporate security, and general management will find it especially informative.

Senior technologists and middle managers with a broad interest in business, and who view technology as a means to attaining business objectives, will find this book equally informative. In many cases, these are the individuals who have brought to light many of the concepts contained in this book. And it is this group, whose members value technology for its vast business utility, that shall find themselves the senior managers of the future.

SCOPE OF DISCUSSION

For most technology consumers, interest in distributed IT resources stops at their own desktops. And for the most part, those consumers who do care avoid thinking about IT resources because the issue is so complex. For those interested and committed few, the process of managing a distributed enterprise of IT assets begins with trying to define the topic. Desktops, servers, bridges, routers, LANs, WANs, protocols, bandwidth, T1 lines, switches, downstream, upstream…these are just a few of the items that make up the distributed IT enterprise. Complicating matters further, each item that makes up this distributed pool of resources has its own set of terms and a self-important view of its role in the enterprise. How then, in a book this size, can one expect to convey any meaningful insight into managing these distributed IT assets? By cheating!

I have chosen to focus on the end point (the end-user desktops and servers) of the distributed enterprise. Although some may view this approach as cheating, in reality it is the quintessential element to managing distributed IT assets. Since the end point is where services are delivered, it is here that organizations can realize the greatest productivity gains. And it is here that the winners are separated from the losers in the race for superior productivity and enhanced bottom lines.

The questions surrounding these end-point assets are basic. What desktops and servers do you have? Where are they located? How are they configured? What is the direction and pace with which they are changing? If you cannot answer these questions, then no matter how well your enterprise is bridged, and no matter how tightly integrated your applications are, you will in the end fail, for it is these desktops and servers that stand between the enterprise and the end user, and between the end user and productivity. Accordingly, this book explores the techniques and opportunities for managing the end point of the distributed IT asset base.

CONCEPTS AND TERMS

The following is a list of concepts and terms that are frequently used in this text.

CLIENTS AND SERVERS

Within the context of this book, clients are the end-user desktops that make up the enterprise. These desktops include the processing units, monitors, a complement of communications hardware and software, operating system software, shrink-wrap (vendor supplied) software, in-house developed software, and attached devices such as a CD-ROM. Servers include the same complement of items as the clients, plus the additional hardware and software that allow them to provide shared services to the client/end-user desktops.

DISTRIBUTED ENTERPRISE (DISTRIBUTED IT ASSETS)

A distributed enterprise is an amalgamation of client and server resources that support the business objectives of the organization. These resources can be actively connected (networked), passively connected (dial-in via a modem), or logically connected (via their utility to the business objectives).

COMMUNICATIONS INFRASTRUCTURE (NETWORK)

The communications infrastructure includes the wires, communications lines, protocols, bridges, routers, and network management services that maintain the actively and passively connected distributed enterprise. Only a small portion of this book deals with the communications infrastructure, and then only as it relates to desktop and server productivity.

POINTS OF CHANGE

Points of change are the changes taking place to the client and server platforms. Since it is not possible to include an explanation of all changes that may affect the enterprise, a list of change sources is included. As this entire text is based on the tracking and management of changes to the distributed IT enterprise, below are some of the sources of change as they relate to this text. Additional information is provided in chapter 12.

• End-user modifications include changes to the operating system configuration, the authorized or unauthorized addition or removal of hardware components or applications, and modifications to applications and services delivered by "corporate."

• Server administrator modifications include the same changes covered under end-user modifications, plus hardware, software, and communications modifications that are unique to the server platform.

• Enterprise-directed modifications include "corporate" changes made to the desktops and servers via electronic software distribution, manually distributed media, or communications reconfigurations.

• Business-directed modifications are a result of changes to business operations. A comprehensive summary of these types of changes is too extensive to list; however, it is important to note that even a seemingly insignificant business-directed modification can have a profound impact on the distributed IT enterprise. Consider, for example, the "cascade effect" of hiring a new employee into a department. In many cases, the new desktop purchased as part of that hire does not go to the new employee, but to the most-senior member of the department. This senior employee, in turn, cascades the old system to the next most-senior member of the department. It is easy to see how the hiring of a single employee can end up changing several dozen desktops.

SETTING THE STAGE

DISTRIBUTED IT RESOURCE MANAGEMENT

The "state of the art" in managing distributed IT assets is presently centered on the ability to collect current IT asset information more frequently and with less effort. Although this is a desirable objective, there is a more advanced generation of solutions which, if understood, can provide business benefits far beyond a timely inventory. The remainder of this chapter contrasts the current "state of the art," an institutional perspective, and a more "visionary" solution for managing the distributed IT asset base.

TRADITIONAL VIEW

Managing a distributed IT asset base is generally synonymous with maintaining an accurate inventory of the desktops and servers. This process is typically accomplished via some combination of electronic discovery and a large group of temporary employees or contractors who gather and consolidate the discovered information on an annual basis. The cost of gathering this information, as detailed in a later chapter, is substantial. These high financial costs, along with the disruption that an inventory causes to end-user productivity, make anything other than annual inventories impractical.

INSTITUTIONAL VIEW

This "once-a-year view" of the distributed IT enterprise, although valuable, is of limited utility. This is why industry experts are presently promoting a new class of asset management software that uses an organization's network to collect and consolidate desktop and server profiles. This new paradigm allows the distributed IT enterprise to be inventoried more frequently and with less end-user disruption. Those advocating this new asset inventory process include it as a peer in an architecture of enterprise management solutions. This architecture is illustrated below:

ENTERPRISE MANAGEMENT			
ASSET MANAGEMENT (INVENTORY) SYSTEMS	APPLICATION CHANGE MANAGEMENT	HELP DESK SYSTEMS	AUTOMATED PURCHASING SYSTEMS
SYSTEMS MANAGEMENT TOOLS	CONFIGURATION CHANGE MANAGEMENT	APPLICATION MANAGEMENT TOOLS	SOFTWARE DISTRIBUTION
ENTERPRISE CHANGE MANAGEMENT	NETWORK MANAGEMENT TOOLS	FIXED ASSET SYSTEMS	OTHERS...

This paradigm is a giant leap forward over traditional methods of managing the distributed IT enterprise because it can provide views of the enterprise on a more frequent basis, with minimal end-user disruption. By having a peer-level facility that provides more current desktop and server information, another layer of depth is added to the management of the enterprise.

A NEW VISION

Although I agree with those calling for more frequent and less labor-intensive views of the enterprise, this is only one step toward effective management of the distributed IT assets.

Arguably, a system that gathers and reports information on the desktop and server complex can be categorized not as a peer, but as an infrastructure for the management of the enterprise. By joining and sharing distributed IT asset information in an open repository, a new infrastructure is created. This infrastructure enables all enterprise management facilities to extend their utility. Further, these management tools can add their unique view of the distributed IT assets to the repository, thereby further enriching each management tool's utility. A diagram highlighting the differences between the institutional view and a new vision for an IT asset repository is illustrated below:

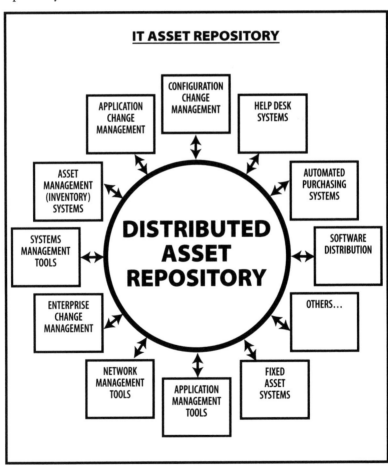

This diagram highlights the two-way communication between the various enterprise tools. For example, the open repository gives the help desk system access to the latest configuration information for a user who is having problems, and it enables a problem history of each individual desktop and server to be added to the repository. The result of this exchange is improved enterprise visibility for all enterprise management functions.

The free flow of information depicted in the diagram is a future goal for many organizations. However, the tools and asset tracking systems that enable such exchanges are available today.

With such an infrastructure in place, applications, tools, and managers can discover the current state of any client or server in the enterprise and how it relates to other enterprise functions. This, however, is only the first step in realizing the full power of the asset repository. By keeping multiple images of each distributed asset configuration over time, regression and sensitivity analyses can be performed on the distributed asset base, thereby extending its utility from an operations tool to a tracking and planning device.

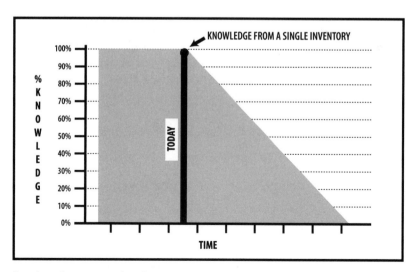

In the above graph, the gray area represents the knowledge base that is available from a system that maintains multiple images of the distributed IT assets over time, while the black line represents the knowledge captured from a current single inventory. The graph highlights the fact that by having a historical base of knowledge, you can gain visibility into the future. This topic is covered in greater detail in later chapters.

Beyond this is the opportunity to provide front-ends to the repository that analyze, track, and report on activities that would otherwise go unnoticed by even the most diligent enterprise staff. As later chapters will illustrate, joining expertise, technology, and a historical base of knowledge allows for the conversion of raw data into valuable insights.

These capabilities are available today to those who understand the benefits of reaching beyond the concept of a simple inventory. Awaiting too are the false starts and dead ends that confront the uninformed. With this in mind, the balance of this book explores the possibilities and pitfalls of creating and leveraging a distributed asset repository.

SUMMARY

Definitions are nothing but hangers that hold our ideas, lest our intellections find themselves in a heap at the bottom of our closet.

CHAPTER 3
• COMPARED TO WHAT? •
COMPARATIVE ANCHORS

Me: How did the calculus exam go?

Mary (my daughter)**:** Great!

Me: What does great mean?

Mary: Upper 2 percent of my class!

Me: What was the class average?

Mary: Thirty-one percent.

Me: And your grade?

Mary: Thirty-eight percent.

Me: Then you failed?

Mary: Yes, but it was a hard test.

This is a fair approximation of a conversation I had with my oldest daughter several years ago. Mary, who is really a very good student, failed to give me the comparative information necessary for me to make an informed assessment of her performance. At Mary's insistence, and in the spirit of full disclosure, the teacher graded on a curve, and Mary got a "D" for her efforts. All of this appears to speak to parenting; however, it holds an equally profound lesson for managing distributed IT assets.

The connection to my daughter's grades can best be illustrated through example. For the purposes of this exercise, assume you have before you a complete audit of all software, hardware, and peripherals that comprise your distributed client/server enterprise. This information is displayed or printed in a manner that allows you to view each machine and its associated assets as a unit, and is cross-tabulated to give you an item count for each type of asset. Further, assume this information was gathered at the exact same instant and is accurate plus or minus 1 percent. No doubt, for most managers this would be a giant step forward in the control of their distributed asset base. In fact, it is nearly a perfect inventory! Well...sounds like we solved this problem; let's get a cold beer and call it a day.

As tempting as that might be, there is a substantial base of evidence that suggests managers are lacking the most critical components of an asset tracking system. Notice the distinction between asset inventory and asset tracking. This distinction results from distributed IT assets having unique qualities that traditional assets (e.g., cars, desks, and machine tools) lack.

Distributed IT assets are constantly undergoing an evolutionary process as software, storage, memory, applications, connectivity, and the computer itself are upgraded, modified, or replaced. Complicating this evolution is the number of sources of change involved, including corporate management information systems (MIS), server administrators, end users, application vendors, and departmental management. In an effort to make sense out of this perpetual migration, forward-thinking professionals use "comparative anchors" to assist in making this evolution both manageable and meaningful.

A comparative anchor is nothing more than a figurative stationary point to which we can tie the ever-evolving asset. In linking an evolving asset to a stationary point, we have the ability to establish the asset's actual position, as well as its relative position to other events and assets that have a convergence of interest.

There are numerous comparative anchors that are indispensable in the management of the enterprise. In the interest of being brief, I have highlighted the anchors that have the broadest applicability to a general audience. Each of these anchors is valuable and can be indispensable in the management of the enterprise. As you study this short list of comparative anchors, keep in mind that the final anchor, "Your Comparative Anchor," offers the greatest potential return on investment (ROI). It is this anchor that allows the assets to be associated with the unique properties of your business operations.

SURVEY OF ANCHORS

TIME COMPARATIVE ANCHOR

The grandest of all comparative anchors is time. Because assets are forever changing and evolving, time becomes the most informative element in the tracking of distributed IT assets. The case studies presented in later chapters highlight the power of a time-based analysis. However, for now, consider the following examples: A CFO can view the value of the IT assets as of a specific date. A help desk analyst can view a snapshot (i.e., a stored inventory for a particular moment in time) of a workstation before and after an end-user problem occurs. A purchasing executive can determine a license count for a specific software application as of a given point in time. Each of these inventories becomes meaningful as a result of being "time anchored."

TRENDS COMPARATIVE ANCHOR

Russell Hoban wrote in *The Lion of Boaz-Jachin*, "If the past cannot teach the present and the father cannot teach the son, then history need not have bothered to go on, and the world has wasted a great deal of time." If we, as senior managers and executives, are to avoid wasting time in the management of the IT asset base, then we must regard and use trending as one of our primary weapons. Actually, trending is a by-product of the Time Comparative Anchor in that it acts as a type of radar. Trending reports on the movement, speed, and direction of the changing distributed IT asset base. This radar is nothing more than plotting the same asset point over multiple time periods and ascertaining its rate of change and future direction.

Consider a CFO who has the ability to predict the desktop turnover rate and, thus, improve overall cash management. Or, consider an IT executive who can accurately predict a usage trend for a particular software application before beginning negotiations with the application vendor. How about a purchasing executive who, by using trend analysis, can determine when users will run out of disk space, allowing for favorable volume purchasing decisions? The Trends Comparative Anchor allows us to use the past and present to better forecast the future.

Phantom Comparative Anchor

Some of the most powerful comparative anchors are neither other assets nor time. These Phantom Comparative Anchors are tags, knowledge, or some type of organization identifier that is associated with the asset. In our "nearly perfect" inventory scenario presented earlier, we had all the "physical information" about our distributed IT asset base; however, the usefulness of this information, without Phantom Comparative Anchors, is limited. Consider the improved utility of this same data if these physical assets are associated with a specific employee, phone number, address, building, department, job title, manager, general ledger account, or priority code. None of these Phantom Comparative Anchors has value in themselves. But, when Phantom Comparative Anchors are combined with the inventory data and historical snapshots, they become powerful tools in managing not just the enterprise, but the entire business process.

My favorite quote regarding the value of Phantom Comparative Anchors comes from an MIS director who was faced with the rather mundane task of upgrading the software in the finance department. He exclaimed, "I can track every desktop down to a specific network address. I get an update on every desktop configuration twice a year, and I know the names and locations of every employee in this company…. But tell you which desktops and servers belong to the finance department? Forget it!" Phantom Comparative Anchors give dimension to an otherwise flat base of asset information.

NULL COMPARATIVE ANCHOR

I read in Will Durant's *The Story of Civilization* that the ancient Egyptians, the most advanced culture of their day, ceased progressing because they never developed the mathematical concept of "zero." The Egyptians, in missing zero, lost sustained greatness. Within this irony we discover the value of the Null Comparative Anchor. Sometimes the most valuable information is in knowing something isn't there.

Consider the impact of a business unit manager being alerted that a particular group of workstations is missing the current version of a critical rate table. Or consider the productivity benefits of having a listing of all workstations and servers that do not have the "corporate standard configuration."

Even more interesting results can be attained by combining Time Comparative Anchors with Null Comparative Anchors. By comparing the current snapshot of the desktops with the next most recent snapshot of the same desktops, we can discover which machines have less main memory from one period to the next, less online storage, a missing CD-ROM, etc. At times, the value of knowing what you don't have is greater than the value of counting your possessions.

REFLECTIVE COMPARATIVE ANCHOR

One of my favorite quotes concerning knowledge comes from Denis Diderot, the French philosopher who said, "There are three principal means of acquiring knowledge available to us: observation of nature, reflection, and experimentation. Observation collects facts; reflection combines them; experimentation verifies the result of that combination." The Reflective Comparative Anchor addresses the combination of facts. By reflecting static information off of other bases of knowledge, we gain insight. For example, to know that the number of WordPerfect installations is declining across the enterprise is knowledge; to know that 100 percent of high-end users (knowledge workers) run WordPerfect is insight. There is an infinite number of examples of how combining information sets can lead to profound insight; several case studies are included that highlight the value of such insights.

YOUR COMPARATIVE ANCHOR(S)

One of my most valued customers is a large and very successful insurance company. I have no doubt that this customer, although wholeheartedly endorsing the value of the aforementioned anchors, would identify this final anchor as the most important means of comparison. The reason for elevating the priority of this anchor is based on the leverage a business-specific anchor can provide to the business enterprise.

This insurance company considers its 4,000 independent agents to be a significant part of both the company's business and its IT enterprise. Accordingly, the company supplies its agents with a wealth of software customized to each individual agent. Within this customization is information (making up Your Comparative Anchor) on the type of policies the agent writes, the agent's name, address, performance history, etc. Part of this customer's newly installed asset tracking system allows it to gather the agent information (from the installed customized software) as part of the desktop inventory. By extracting this business information from the supplied software, and tying it to the IT resources (the agents' desktops) that support the mission-critical application, the insurance company is able to provide a superior level of customized support to its agent population. The joining of information resources and business knowledge allows the company to improve the productivity of its agents' policy-writing efforts, and anticipate its agents' technology needs and problems. There is no line between the business enterprise and the technology enterprise; each supports the other by providing insight and productivity gains that are mutually beneficial.

SUMMARY

If you want to know what you have, count it; if you want to know what is happening to it, compare it!

CASE STUDY 1
NOW YOU SEE IT, NOW YOU DON'T

PROLOGUE

XYZ is a large insurance company with forty major field offices in eleven countries. XYZ has a distributed enterprise model that allows for some level of autonomy and buying authority within each geographic location, business unit, and functional department. The responsibility for managing and supporting the distributed enterprise falls under the information technology group, which is headed by a CIO.

ENTERPRISE DEFINITION

XYZ's distributed enterprise includes approximately 30,000 desktops, which are supported by 2,700 servers. Three different server platforms and four desktop platforms are supported. The enterprise is geographically dispersed with large groups of users in Chicago, London, Boston, and San Francisco.

THE SITUATION/PROBLEM

The company recently developed, and plans to put into production within thirty days, a major financial consolidation system that involves all of the distributed desktops within the finance department. During a trip to several of the major field locations to check on the progress of the implementation, the CIO requests a demonstration of the new system. In Chicago, the field agent giving the demonstration encounters an "out-of-main-memory condition" that prohibits the completion of the demonstration. A quick analysis indicates the affected system does not have the required complement of memory to run the application, even though all systems were supposed to have been upgraded to the requisite configuration thirty days earlier. The CIO makes a note of the agent's name and network address and continues his tour.

The First Step

Knowing that all 2,900 Chicago desktops targeted to support the new financial consolidation system were scheduled for a memory upgrade to be completed thirty days ago, the CIO queries the asset tracking system to determine which of these do not have the proper memory configuration. The latest snapshot of the systems in question shows that 280 of the 2,900 systems do not have the required sixteen megabytes (MB) of main memory. The CIO runs a report identifying the desktops requiring a memory upgrade to support the new application and an effort begins to upgrade the deficient systems.

Here we see the power of having an up-to-date inventory of the distributed enterprise. The deficient desktops scheduled to go into production in less than thirty days are identified before they fail, and remedial action is taken. Even if the CIO had not noticed the glitch, standard procedures can enforce a final check of all targeted systems before the new software is deployed. All of this speaks to the power of having a current inventory, but much more can be learned as the CIO begins to leverage the historical information available from the asset tracking system.

Tracking Down a Problem

With a plan in place to correct the memory deficiency, the CIO turns his attention to the more strategic question: Which of the 2,900 Chicago desktops targeted for the memory upgrade were actually upgraded to the prerequisite configuration thirty days ago as planned? To his surprise, all 2,900 desktops reported having memory upgraded for the new financial consolidation system by the designated date. A specific check of the system that failed during the demonstration shows that thirty days earlier it too reported a full memory complement.

Somewhat perplexed by these asset changes, the CIO runs an enterprise-wide Suspicious Activity Analysis. There are several sections to this analysis, each providing its own insight into the source of the problem. *Note: Although such an analysis would ideally appear on a single page, this chapter presents the sections in a series.*

SUSPICIOUS ACTIVITY ANALYSIS

SUSPICIOUS ACTIVITY ANALYSIS – SUMMARY

The first section of this analysis provides a framework for understanding the other sections of the report.

SUMMARY

An analysis of the 30,114 desktops tracked during the period ending 3/15 reveals 2,264 suspicious activities. Of these, 977 are desktops that failed to report within 7 days of their scheduled inventories, 578 show a decline in the number of hard disks, 690 show a decline in memory, and 19 are missing a CD-ROM.

The total number of suspicious activities is 70 percent greater than the previous month.

SUSPICIOUS ACTIVITY ANALYSIS – DEPARTMENTAL BREAKDOWN

The second section of this report takes the Summary and breaks it down by functional business units.

The insight derived from the table on the next page begins with the far right column, "% of Enterprise." This information provides XYZ's CIO with a frame of reference when examining the various departmental counts (four center columns, shaded) of suspicious activity. The CIO notices in the first row that finance has 23 percent of all enterprise desktops, but appears to have a disproportionate number of desktops (540) reporting a decrease in main memory.

DEPARTMENT	NOT REPORTING	DECLINE IN MEMORY	DECLINE IN HARD DISKS	MISSING CD-ROMs	% OF ENTERPRISE
FINANCE	118	540	136	0	23%
MARKETING	128	80	129	0	16%
SALES	232	46	99	0	27%
ACTUARIAL	410	21	109	19	16%
OTHER	89	3	105	0	18%
TOTAL	**977**	**690**	**578**	**19**	**100%**

SUSPICIOUS ACTIVITY ANALYSIS – SNAPSHOTS OVER TIME

The third section of the analysis enriches each element by presenting it in a historical context and graphically displaying its speed and direction (trend).

The information provided in the Departmental Breakdown, although significant, does not tell a complete story. To fully comprehend the significance of the numbers in the table, they must be examined within the context of time. To assist in this examination, the analysis includes a trend analysis for each element. Each of these analyses plots a specific type of suspicious activity over time. A table of numerical values represented in the charts is summarized below:

	1/1	1/15	2/1	2/15	3/1	3/15
NOT REPORTING	676	600	519	630	625	977
DECLINE IN MEMORY	180	585	156	141	163	690
DECLINE IN HARD DISKS	218	355	410	489	535	578
MISSING CD-ROMs	0	0	1	3	8	19

SUSPICIOUS ACTIVITY ANALYSIS – DESKTOPS NOT REPORTING

The following graph plots the number of desktops not reporting (i.e., updating the repository with a new snapshot of the desktop) on the scheduled date for the past six snapshot periods. Note: In this case the snapshots were taken every two weeks.

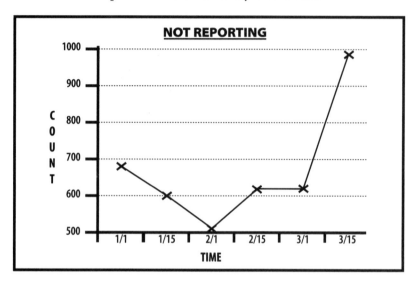

When examining the Desktops Not Reporting graph, the CIO notices an unusual spike not apparent when reviewing the finance department on the Departmental Breakdown. In referring back to the breakdown table, he discovers the problem is centered in the actuarial department (with 410 desktops not reporting), which causes him to initiate an investigation.

SUSPICIOUS ACTIVITY ANALYSIS –
DECLINE IN MEMORY

Temporarily setting aside the issue of Desktops Not Reporting, the CIO turns to the next trend analysis, Decline in Memory. Here, there is a strong indication that some form of undesirable activity is linked to the failed software demonstration in Chicago.

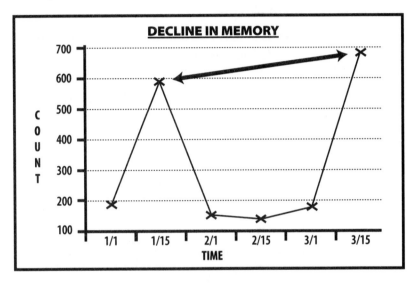

In examining the above graph, the CIO notices spikes in main memory decline for the snapshot periods of 1/15 and 3/15 (arrows) indicating there may be some outside element involved. The CIO makes a copy of the Suspicious Activity Analysis and sends it, along with a detailed listing of affected users, departments, and locations, to corporate security.

SUSPICIOUS ACTIVITY ANALYSIS – DECLINE IN HARD DISKS

When looking at the Departmental Breakdown, the "Decline in Hard Disks" column does not show any unusual distribution between departments and, therefore, receives little of the CIO's attention. In examining this element over time, however, the CIO gains an unsettling insight.

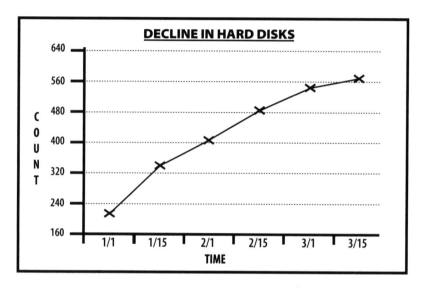

According to the above graph, the number of desktops experiencing a decrease in hard disk capacity has nearly tripled over the past six snapshot periods. This trend and the supporting details are also sent to corporate security for investigation.

Suspicious Activity Analysis – Missing CD-ROMs

The last element in the analysis, Missing CD-ROMs, also has no relevance to the initial investigation, as the finance department reported no occurrence of this type of suspicious activity. However, the CIO discovers an undesirable upward trend in missing CD-ROMs for the corporation overall. With a look back at the Departmental Breakdown, he realizes that this trend can be tied back to the actuarial department.

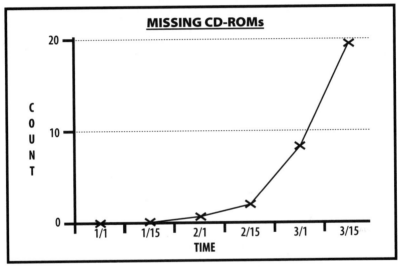

Because of the small numbers involved (nineteen missing CD-ROMs on 3/15), and because of a close working relationship, the CIO places a call to the vice president in charge of the actuarial department. As a result, the vice president requests a report detailing the users involved; he then initiates an informal investigation.

Epilogue

An epilogue is included in this hypothetical case study to highlight some of the discoveries that MIS professionals have shared with me in the management of their distributed enterprise.

As a result of the CIO's investigation of the anomalies highlighted in the Suspicious Activity Analysis, it is learned that:

• The two spikes in Decline in Memory coincide with the use of a specific contractor hired to perform data entry during off hours. In both cases, this contractor was employed in the finance department during the time period when main memory chips were removed from the desktops. The various purchasing agencies are notified, and the vendor is suspended pending further investigation.

• The Decline in Hard Disks proves to be a broader problem. Corporate security, by tracking a serial number in a lower capacity drive, discovers that a small but increasing percentage of employees have been removing the small-capacity drives from their personal home systems and swapping them with the larger-capacity drives on their office desktops. These employees are "counseled," and corporate security initiates a campaign to inform all employees that such activity will be closely monitored in the future.

• The Missing CD-ROM investigation proves to be less dramatic. Some employees in the actuarial department, while working on a large project with a tight deadline, were permitted to remove their external CD-ROM drive and use it at home over the weekend. The snapshot, which was taken early Monday morning, detected those drives that had not yet been reconnected. The policy that allows employees, in an effort to meet corporate deadlines, to take equipment home over the weekend also explains the large number of Desktops Not Reporting. XYZ institutes a formal sign-out policy that enables the tracking of equipment that leaves the premises.

From Theory to Application

This case study highlights the utility of the seemingly academic concepts covered at the beginning of this chapter. The Time Comparative Anchor is necessary to establish that the upgrades had been performed on schedule and that the memory deficient desktops were more than just an oversight. The Trends Comparative Anchor allows the CIO to quantify the nature and severity of the problem. The Phantom Comparative Anchor permits the association of assets to departments and users. The Null Comparative Anchor is the basis for the entire analysis in that it highlights missing elements. And finally, the Reflective Comparative Anchor not only enables a comparison between departments, but also allows the CIO to compare departmental counts against their percentage representation within the enterprise.

CHAPTER 4

• WHO NEEDS IT ANYWAY? •

BUSINESS BENEFITS OF ASSET TRACKING

Me: Excuse me, I heard that the heavy snow has the ramp to the tunnel blocked. Can you tell me another route to Logan Airport?

Hotel Clerk: Here, I have a map. Let me show you. *(Clerk gives me a map.)*

Me: *(After driving eight miles in three hours only to find the airport closed)* I need a room—the airport is closed until tomorrow.

Hotel Clerk: Yeah, I thought it was funny that you were in such a hurry to get there.... Sorry, we're all booked up.

Me: You mean when you gave me directions, you knew the airport was closed?

Hotel Clerk: Sure did.

Me: WHY DIDN'T YOU TELL ME?

Hotel Clerk: It didn't seem important to you.

Here is an experience that taught me three valuable lessons. First, not all hotel clerks are working to fund an education in rocket science. Second, never, never, never give up a hotel room in a snowstorm. Third, sometimes we, and others, do not know what we need. Now, although I am tempted to write this chapter on the second of these lessons—since spending the night at the airport trying to sleep in a phone booth cubicle provides a world of instruction—I have elected to focus on the third.

Oftentimes in our intimate understanding of a topic, we fail to see the utility of our knowledge beyond the scope of our own needs. IT professionals and other decision makers who undertake the task of actively tracking the distributed enterprise are consistently surprised by the broad application of the information and analysis that results from even the most basic asset tracking system. Clearly, if all the utility of an asset tracking system were known in advance of their efforts, IT professionals would have designed a more flexible and forward-thinking solution. The remainder of this chapter describes the application of asset tracking data across departmental boundaries. It is in considering these "milestones of utility" that we have the best opportunity to build a tracking solution that tells the rest of the world, "By the way, did you know the airport is closed until tomorrow morning?"

The following presents a brief survey of the utility of asset tracking across seven business units. It is not intended to be an exhaustive list of either functionality or scope. I chose these departments and these examples as a means of opening up the universe, not defining the city limits. And if you ask yourself as you read this, "Why didn't he include this?" or "How could he omit a discussion of that?" then I have accomplished my task, as you have already begun to expand the universe of utility provided by an asset tracking solution.

FINANCE

When we first think of asset tracking within the context of the finance department, we think of a year-end physical inventory. There are many studies of how much it costs to inventory distributed IT assets, ranging from $60 per seat to $120 per seat. Clearly, some form of automated inventory would go a long way toward paying for an asset tracking system. There is, however, a broader set of questions we must consider if we are to view asset tracking from a financial perspective, including some form of automated reconciliation with the existing fixed-asset accounting system. Any links or automated functions that enable the tracking system to match and report variances between what it finds and what is being carried on the books can, over time, improve both the accuracy of what is reported and the bottom line.

Consider the reconciliation of the fixed-asset accounting system with the current information reported by the asset tracking system. A single line from such a report might disclose that the fixed-asset accounting system lists 3,814 Pentium-class machines in service, while the tracking system found only 114 such machines attached to the network! This brings to mind a long list of questions, including: Where are the other 3,700 machines? How do we account for the remaining useful life of the 3,700 machines? Is it financially advantageous to give them to charity? If we can find them, what is it costing to store them and to insure them? All of these questions, and many more, will go unanswered until such a reconciliation is performed.

Financial managers have the burden of tracking assets, costs, and revenues across time and organizations. For the most part, this is accomplished via the comparison of a plan or schedule to actual results. Unfortunately, the process of tracking and reporting on the value, cost, and utility of distributed IT assets presents challenges that are not encountered when doing the same for a dump truck. IT assets are slippery; they get reassigned, upgraded, retired, folded, spindled, and mutilated. Trying to maintain control of these resources without an asset tracking system is a frustrating and expensive undertaking. Undaunted nonetheless, financial professionals continue their efforts because they understand that maintaining control over the value, acquisition, and disposition of IT assets can substantially improve the financial performance of their organization. Even with this effort, finance professionals frequently don't discover large variances between their fixed-asset accounting system and what is actually in the enterprise until the year-end physical inventory.

With this in mind, consider the value of a monthly analysis showing the IT asset base assigned to the sales department that graphically tracks desktops by processor type across an eight-quarter period. Or consider a simple exception report that provides a monthly departmental breakdown of discovered assets that were not in the previous month's snapshot. Perhaps sorting these new assets by the responsible manager would be useful. To a financial manager struggling to produce an annual inventory, these reports seem impossible, yet they are an effortless by-product of a full-featured asset tracking system.

PURCHASING

Although technically part of the finance department, the purchasing department has a unique perspective—it is responsible for spending the organization's money. And with this charter comes the responsibility of spending it in a manner that optimizes the organization's return on investment.

One of the primary tools the purchasing department uses to carry out its charter is vendor negotiations. For example, a purchasing executive might call in the representative of Clyde's Trucks and say, "Look Clyde, we have 200 of your trucks, and we are projecting a need for fifty-five more. Now what kind of deal will you give me?" On the other hand, the purchasing executive is just as likely to get a call from Clyde announcing that there is a new engine modification available at a very attractive price. In either case, the purchasing executive needs to know the same baseline information. How many Clyde trucks do they own? How many are in service? Are the primary users happy with Clyde's trucks?

Let's switch gears (no pun intended) and consider the same exercise, but now the purchasing executive is dealing with Spreadsheet

Inc. instead of Clyde's Trucks. Spreadsheet Inc.'s records show that the company owns 11,450 copies of its product. Spreadsheet Inc. makes a very powerful argument that the installed version of its product is outdated, harder to use, less powerful, and more difficult to support. Out of the kindness of its heart, Spreadsheet Inc. offers to discount the upgrade price from $99 down to $49 if the company agrees to upgrade all copies.

Sounds like a good deal, right? Maybe it is, maybe it's not—but you can't know unless you are tracking your IT assets. A single query uncovers that only 3,700 of the 11,450 copies of Spreadsheet Inc.'s package are installed on the desktops, and even if you had to pay full price for the 3,700 copies, it would still be more cost-effective than signing up for 11,450 copies at the attractive $49 price.

After re-focusing negotiations with Spreadsheet Inc. around the correct number of copies, the purchasing executive turns his attention to a product/vendor analysis. He runs a report showing that of the 3,700 installed copies of the Spreadsheet Inc. product, 2,100 copies are installed in the marketing department. In response to this high percentage of use, the purchasing executive places a telephone call to the IT manager responsible for the marketing department, and informs her of the proposed advantages of the upgrade. The offer receives a less-than-enthusiastic reception as the proposed upgrade does not address a major compatibility problem that marketing is experiencing when using the Spreadsheet Inc. product with other applications. When informed of this, the Spreadsheet Inc. representative indicates that the compatibility issue is addressed in the next revision, and offers to supply the future release at no additional cost.

With this information in hand, the purchasing executive decides to make one more check before conducting price negotiations. He generates a report showing, by department, the number of installed copies of the product at the beginning of each of the past six quarters. The analysis shows a steady downward trend across the company in the use of the product. Further, the marketing department shows the steepest decline in use. With this information, the purchasing decision is postponed, and the company conducts an analysis to identify what application and which vendor should replace the Spreadsheet Inc. product.

GENERAL MANAGEMENT

General management's use of an asset tracking system is centered around the organization as a whole. For example, if a company is positioning itself to be acquired or is considering a merger, expansion, downsizing, or expansion through acquisition, then being able to accurately track the number, value, and location of the distributed IT assets would provide significant benefits.

If a company is considering a major expansion, it needs to define the IT infrastructure required to facilitate and support the expansion. To develop an expansion plan, the company must answer several questions: What is the average number of employees per desktop system for each department? What is the average configuration for each department? And, what are the incremental transition costs of the plan?

If a company is planning to downsize, several asset protection and disposal questions must be addressed: What assets will be idle? How can they be redeployed? What surplus assets will we have? What is the value of the surplus assets? Where are the surplus assets located? And, how do we protect them during the downsizing turmoil?

An asset tracking system can also be a valuable tool to facilitate mergers and acquisitions. Companies that frequently entertain acquisitions can require a target company to implement an asset tracking system as part of the due diligence effort. Once installed, the system establishes a benchmark of IT assets at the organization being acquired, preventing assets from "getting lost" during the consolidation, and giving the acquiring IT group a detailed blueprint of the soon-to-be-merged base of technology.

OPERATIONS

For the purposes of this discussion, the overall management of the distributed IT enterprise has been included under the general heading "Operations." This function is usually the responsibility of an IT executive that neither had, nor has, any form of absolute control over the current or future disposition of the distributed enterprise. Yet within these obvious constraints, this brave soul is held accountable for the successful operation of these same resources.

Within the madness of this assignment, a functioning asset tracking system can be a primary link to sanity. For example, a simple request to upgrade all of the marketing department to the latest version of its word processing package comes to the operations executive. Purchasing informs him that the upgrade fee will be $50 per workstation, and that 2,300 workstations need the upgrade. In theory, all that is required is a quick check of the budget to see if marketing has the $115,000 for the upgrade, and the software is ordered.

The French philosopher Voltaire may have had the heart of an IT executive in charge of the distributed enterprise, for he wrote, "Let us work without theorizing, 'tis the only way to make life endurable." Taking Voltaire's lead, the IT executive in the example above will not order the software upgrade until he performs a basic analysis. The questions that need to be answered include: What are the prerequisites for the proposed software upgrade? How many of the workstations do not have the required processor, operating system, memory, or disk space to use the proposed software? What is the cost of upgrading the workstations that do not meet the prerequisites? Without answers to these and other questions, the approval of the upgrade could cascade into a budget crisis, an end-user productivity issue, help desk overload, and a substantial expenditure of IT resources to untangle this string of events. The case study at the conclusion of this chapter graphically illustrates this example.

If the IT executive is to keep even the smallest portion of his or her sanity, then a crystal ball is required. Small insights into the future are critical to keeping the enterprise fully operational. For example, knowing when a file server is within two weeks of exceeding its storage capacity (based on past usage) allows the IT executive to eliminate a production problem before it takes place. Or, when reading in the press that a certain combination of hardware, operating system version, and application can cause problems, the asset tracking system can isolate affected desktops and servers and enable the company to apply a fix before the problem is even encountered.

One of the tools that is part of any attempt to manage the distributed enterprise is electronic software distribution. Electronic software distribution has the ability to make uniform changes across a distributed base of IT assets. There are problems in paradise, however, because—with few exceptions—the enterprise contains desktops with diverse configurations. The challenge then becomes how to prepare distribution packages that address the unique configuration groups within the enterprise. With an asset tracking system, the company can create lists of desktops that meet the prerequisites for a targeted distribution, thereby dramatically reducing the number of failed distributions. Further, by modeling the distribution against the asset tracking repository, variances in configurations can be identified, and packages can be adjusted accordingly.

An asset tracking solution is equally useful to an operations executive who is attempting to maintain a desktop standard. The solution can automatically, or on demand, report any variances from the desired standard configuration or any conditions that may be considered harmful to the desktop.

BUSINESS MANAGEMENT

It may seem like a stretch to include business management as a topic of discussion for an asset tracking system, but consider the following examples before dismissing the possibilities.

A module on the desktop "wakes up" and asks the user to supply information, such as the tag number on the side of the personal computer (PC) or the brand name of the monitor. Taking the concept a step further, the desktop could report the number of records entered in a specific file as a means of determining a data entry clerk's productivity. This information is stored in the asset tracking database along with the user's name, department number, central processing unit (CPU) type, etc., and it is accessed as easily as any other configuration information.

A full-featured asset tracking system can also track non-IT assets that are logically associated with a specific desktop. Desks, chairs, telephones, and fax machines are just a few of the items that can potentially be tracked as part of the distributed enterprise.

A dynamic asset tracking system has the ability to associate any information with a logical desktop. By relating user information (e.g., fax number, mailing address, e-mail address, department, division, employee number, etc.) to the desktop configuration information, the company can establish a virtual link with its personnel via its distributed IT asset repository.

CORPORATE SECURITY

Protecting company assets is often the responsibility of the corporate security department. One of the most difficult tasks corporate security encounters is the protection of the highly liquid, dispersed, and evolving materials that comprise the distributed IT asset base. The mission of corporate security is not to solve crimes, but to maintain a strong presence that discourages illegal acts. An asset tracking system can flag any server or desktop that fails to make a regular report, as well as those machines that report a missing component. This alert system allows corporate security to be highly visible to all corporate locations by responding to missing assets in a timely manner.

To a security officer, it makes little difference whether the asset was stolen or sent out for repair; the important thing is that those who have access to the asset (employees, contractors, cleaning staff, etc.) are aware that the asset is being tracked and will be promptly discovered when missing. Knowledge that assets are being monitored serves as a strong deterrent to theft.

One of my customers was encouraged to install an asset tracking system after discovering a substantial theft of memory chips and hard disks. The thieves were removing higher-capacity memory chips and disk drives from the desktops and replacing them with lower-capacity components. An active asset tracking system (using Time, Trends, and Null Comparative Anchors) can point corporate security officers to those desktops experiencing reduced configurations. Some of the conditions that can be detected include systems failing to report from one scheduled snapshot to the next, reduced main memory and hard disk storage, and missing communications adapters, video cards, and CD-ROM drives.

CUSTOMER SERVICE/HELP DESK

Most successful IT professionals consider the end-user's time to be their most valued asset. Accordingly, they spend many sleepless hours worrying about how to make the distributed enterprise as productive as possible for the end user. A vice president of a major bank once did the arithmetic for me. He said, "I am responsible for providing desktop technology to 18,000 end users. Fully loaded, each user costs the bank about $105 per hour. Now, if I tie up each of my end users for just one hour per month with non-productive technology issues, it costs the bank $1.89 million." With this idea in mind, most major enterprises have established help desk functions in an effort to quickly remove any IT-related obstacles to end-user productivity. An effective asset tracking system can substantially aid the help desk function by reducing the time it takes to solve end-user problems.

Consider the following example. An end user calls the help desk and gives his first and last name. The help desk professional enters the name into the help desk system, which is linked to an asset tracking repository. Immediately the end-user's name, network address, mailing address, phone number, fax number, and basic system information appear on the screen. The help desk professional asks the end user for the date the problem first appeared and enters it into the asset tracking system.

The asset tracking system immediately displays the deltas between the last known time the end-user's desktop was fully operational and the most recent snapshot of the desktop. The deltas that are displayed include changes in hardware, configuration files, applications installed, and applications deleted. The help desk professional is presented only with the information that has changed, and does not have to wade through a full report on the desktop. By focusing all parties on only those items that were altered, the asset tracking system improves both the productivity of the end user and the help desk professional.

Another advantage offered by an active asset tracking system is that it enables the help desk professional to leverage the knowledge gained through correcting a problem. In the above help desk example, assume the help desk professional determines that the problem is a combination of an older operating system version (3.1) in conflict with a new application version (6.0). Querying the asset tracking system, the help desk professional can do a quick analysis of all desktops that meet the problem criteria and inform the users of potential problems before they occur. A plan could then be implemented to correct the configuration anomaly.

If the help desk group wants to be more aggressive in preventing problems, it could run an asset tracking analysis to identify those users who are migrating toward the problem (i.e., those running operating system revision 3.1 and application version 5.0). Once found, the help desk would inform users that upgrading their application to 6.0 also requires an operating system upgrade.

LEGAL

An active asset tracking system is a strong indicator to both internal (employees) and external (the Software Publishers Association) sources that you are serious about license compliance. It also delivers the added benefit, should you ever be audited, of providing you with a definitive understanding of all license obligations.

By combining purchasing records and asset tracking information, you can highlight possible license violations before they become an issue. Those conducting such an analysis are often pleasantly surprised to learn that although the company or department is underlicensed on the latest version of a specific package, they are substantially overlicensed on a slightly older revision of the application. In fact, asset tracking systems often find a substantial number of users who have multiple versions of an application installed on the same desktop. Painless compliance is often possible by shifting these slightly older revisions to users who do not require the latest version of an application.

Another legal application of an asset tracking solution concerns the use of the World Wide Web (WWW). There is currently a substantial amount of legal activity centered around employees being exposed to sexually explicit material that is downloaded from the WWW by a manager or co-worker. In chapter 9, we will explore how an effective asset tracking system can detect and prevent such legal liability.

SUMMARY

In better understanding the topic, I built a better mousetrap; in sharing that base of knowledge, I built a better world.

CASE STUDY 2
THE BIG PICTURE

Prologue

ABC Software is a large developer of computer software. It has tight purchasing policies and procedures that are based on a central buying authority. ABC Software primarily relies on acquisitions for its growth, averaging three major acquisitions per year. The general managers of the eleven divisions, and their respective IT professionals, manage the day-to-day operations of division enterprises, including the acquisition of IT resources. A corporate MIS staff, headed by the vice president of information technology, is responsible for the overall design, implementation, and delivery of corporate-wide enterprise services.

Enterprise Definition

ABC Software's distributed enterprise consists of 23,000 desktops, supported by 2,000 servers. The largest concentration of desktops and servers (28 percent) is installed at corporate headquarters. The balance of equipment is located at division headquarters (44 percent) and at various field locations (28 percent).

The Situation/Problem

ABC Software runs its business via the distributed enterprise. Applications include e-mail, order entry, product development, product testing, accounting, revenue forecasts, proposal generation, and hundreds of other applications that rely on the enterprise to share and consolidate information. With this dependence comes the challenge of keeping the various divisions, departments, and geographic locations synchronized as they experience varying rates of growth and as they adopt diverse technologies.

If ABC Software is to continue its rapid pace of expansion and its dependence on the distributed enterprise, a means must be found to bring an enterprise vision to the various senior managers within the divisions. These autonomous managers must be convinced that by considering the enterprise beyond their own boundaries, they too can be better served. To succeed, ABC Software must establish the enterprise as an entity that transcends individual departments or divisions.

THREE-STEP PROCESS

Before introducing the senior management team to the problems and dynamics of the corporate enterprise, care must be taken first to level set their knowledge of their own organizations. This requires, for some period of time, that managers be given a concise and consistent analysis of the IT resources in their divisional enterprises. The format of this analysis should be constant across all divisions.

Once this analysis has been distributed on a regular basis (e.g., semimonthly over a one-year period), managers are encouraged to look for trends within their divisions.

The final step is to compare and contrast trends of various divisional enterprises to each other and against the business plans of those business units and the corporation as a whole.

THE ANALYSIS

It is critical that the analysis be easily "digested" and presented on a single page so the results can be compared over time. For instance, managers can lay out six of these one-page, easy-to-interpret analyses end to end to obtain an immediate view of asset trends during the past six months across their organization. Multiple-page reports or tedious reporting methods inhibit this type of trend analysis.

A nearly ideal analysis that compares a specified division to the entire corporation is described on the following pages. There are five sections to this report, each providing its own insight into the subenterprise. *Note: Although such a report would ideally appear on a single page, this chapter presents the sections in a series.*

IT ASSET ALLOCATION ANALYSIS: LAN PRODUCTS DIVISION

IT ASSET ALLOCATION ANALYSIS – SUMMARY

The first section provides a framework for understanding the remaining sections.

SUMMARY

There are 4,118 workstations in the LAN Products Division supported by 275 servers. The workstations have a total of 2,471 GB of hard disk storage, of which 82 percent is used, leaving 18 percent available for future use. The servers have a total of 1,100 GB of hard disk storage, of which 73 percent is used, leaving 27 percent available for future use.

The average workstation has 600 MB of hard disk storage and is at 82 percent of capacity. The average server has 4,000 MB of hard disk storage and is at 73 percent of capacity.

There is, on average, a minus 4 MB difference in installed RAM and a minus 95 MB difference in hard disk storage between the LAN Products Division and the remainder of the corporation.

IT ASSET ALLOCATION ANALYSIS – OPERATING SYSTEM DISTRIBUTION

The second section of the analysis presents the division management with the broadest measurement of desktop utility—the operating system.

The following graph establishes the distribution of operating systems within the division and, as a point of reference (Reflective Comparative Anchor), contrasts this distribution against the balance of the corporation.

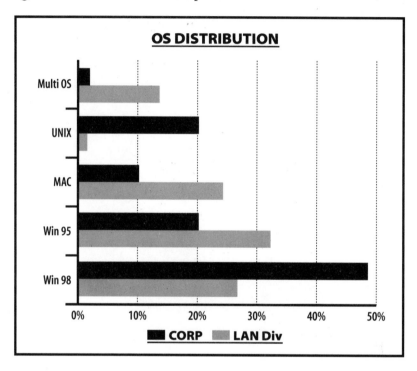

In examining this second section, the business unit executive may, for the first time, gain a broad understanding of the division's technology base and how it blends with the rest of the corporate enterprise. Questions that are raised after just a brief review of the above chart include: Why are so many of the LAN products division's workstations carrying the overhead of multiple operating systems? Are there benefits to using UNIX that the LAN products division is not aware of? What makes us so dependent on the Macintosh platform? And, why is the LAN products division's migration from Windows 95 to Windows 98 so far behind the rest of the corporation?

IT ASSET ALLOCATION ANALYSIS –
TOP APPLICATIONS DISTRIBUTION

The third section of the analysis answers the obvious question generated by the previous chart—how are the workstation resources actually being used?

Usually once the technology platform is understood, questions turn to how the workstations are being used. This information is graphically displayed, again contrasting the LAN products division with the balance of the corporation.

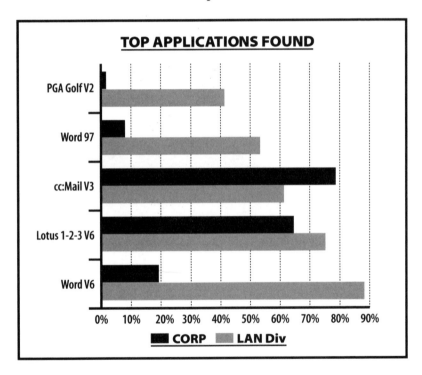

Once you know what applications populate the desktops, you can understand the utility of the desktops and you can understand the application compatibility between users. This will help you more effectively plan hardware and software upgrades. Questions that might follow a brief review of the previous chart include: What does PGA Golf have to do with the mission of this division? Why are we running two versions of Word? And, what is the corporation using for word processing? Considering that a large number of desktops have two word processors and PGA Golf installed, is the proposed disk upgrade really necessary?

IT ASSET ALLOCATION ANALYSIS – CPU DISTRIBUTION

The fourth section of the analysis anchors the operating system and application sections to the base of hardware technology.

By examining the previous two sections of the analysis in light of the installed base of hardware technology, we can begin to establish a "cause and effect relationship" between the various components of the desktop enterprise.

As we saw earlier, the LAN products division is substantially behind the rest of the corporation in upgrading to new operating system versions. It also appears that the LAN products division is out of step in its selection of a word processing standard. These anomalies could be the result of business practices, or they could be tied to the limitations of the hardware platforms. If, for example, Windows 98 required a faster processor than was installed across the division, a natural consequence of having the slower base of processors would be to run older versions of less resource-intensive software.

The following chart highlights the fact that the LAN products division is behind in adopting new hardware technology as well.

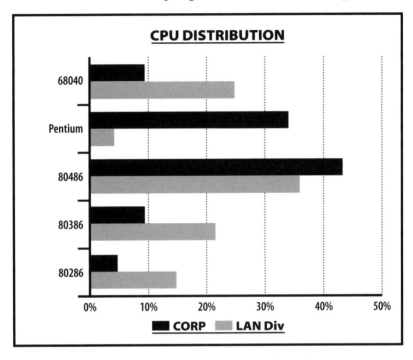

The fundamental question: Is the LAN products division running older technology because its application base does not require additional processor capacity, or is it missing out on the end-user productivity gained through installing the latest software revisions because of hardware restrictions?

Before studying the impact of processor capacity on business productivity, a broad understanding of other "technology gateways" is required. Often the capacity of the desktop is limited by factors not related to processor speed. The final two sections of this analysis highlight these factors.

IT ASSET ALLOCATION ANALYSIS – RAM CAPACITY

The fifth section of this analysis highlights how much random access memory (RAM) is installed on the LAN products division's desktops, and contrasts it with the corporation desktops. This is especially important as many applications, and/or combinations of applications, require a certain amount of RAM.

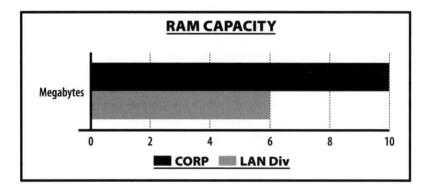

The above graph continues to highlight the fact that the LAN products division has substantially fewer capable desktops when compared to the rest of the corporation. This may be the result of not needing additional memory to run the desired complement of applications, the fact that the installed CPU base does not support additional RAM, or budget considerations. Regardless of the reason, knowing the RAM complement can be invaluable as additional applications, corporate or division inspired, are considered.

IT ASSET ALLOCATION ANALYSIS — HARD DISK CAPACITY

The last section of this analysis highlights the status of hard disk storage for the LAN products division's desktops.

Hard disk storage is important because all desktop applications that are resident on the desktop consume disk space and require some form of "working margin" to complete their tasks. In addition, considering the declining prices of online storage, it is rarely cost-efficient to burden end users with the task of juggling limited storage capacity.

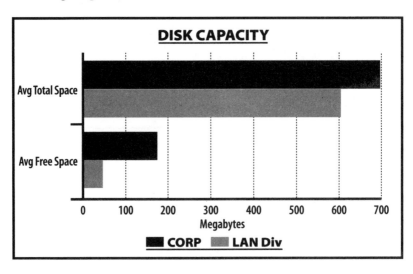

The above graph follows the earlier trends in that the LAN products division is again underconfigured when compared to the rest of the corporate enterprise. Of greater interest than the average hard disk capacity is the delta in free space available between the LAN products division and the corporation. Should the corporation want to distribute an application or data file to the enterprise that requires ninety megabytes of hard disk space, the LAN products division would find its technology base awkwardly out of step with the rest of the enterprise.

Building Enterprise Knowledge

Providing the senior management team of ABC's LAN products division with the above analysis has given team members new insight into the composition, application, and risks associated with their enterprise configuration. As mentioned earlier, all of the sections of this analysis would ideally appear on a single page. With such a consolidation (see the figure below), over time, the management of the LAN products division can gain insight into their enterprise and how it relates to the corporate enterprise. By regularly running this analysis and posting the results side by side on a wall, trends can easily be identified.

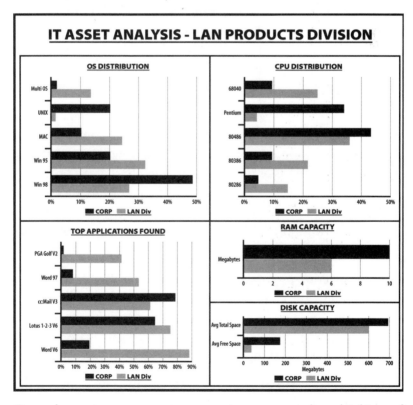

Once the senior management team is accustomed to thinking of its IT asset base as an entity, cross-division sharing of the above analysis can be instituted. This draws all parties closer to recognizing the value of coordinating their efforts, and introduces the corporate enterprise into the divisional IT decision process.

An epilogue is included in this hypothetical case study to highlight some of the discoveries that MIS professionals have shared with me in the management of their distributed enterprise.

As a result of reviewing the IT Asset Allocation Analysis, the LAN products division's management learns that:

• The LAN products division, which was created as the result of several acquisitions, has multiple desktop standards. This partly explains the distribution of operating systems across the LAN products division enterprise. Management forms a task group to investigate the cost and business advantages of standardizing on a single operating system environment.

• The corporation recently negotiated a favorable contract with a leading word processor provider whose product requires fewer resources, has an easier user interface, and offers greater compatibility across platforms than the word processor installed in the LAN products division. As a result, management establishes standards within the LAN products division based on the favorable word processor.

• An investigation prompted by the analysis reveals that more than 80 percent of the employee base has PGA Golf, as well as other games, on their desktops. LAN products division management takes the appropriate action to ensure that all games are removed from employees' desktops.

• The technology gap between the LAN products division and the corporation highlights the fact that the division is falling dangerously behind the technology curve, impacting employee productivity. Therefore, management adjusts the budget to channel more resources into a planned upgrade of the LAN products division enterprise.

FROM THEORY TO APPLICATION

This case study describes a seemingly utopian situation of the division heads lining up behind the natural needs of the corporate enterprise. Before dismissing this possibility, consider the fact that it is in the "selfish" interests of each division to make the "corporate" decisions regarding their individual enterprises. It is by bringing together "pictures" of the individual interests, in a common format to form a picture of the whole, that everyone can share a vision.

Consider how the above concept might fit into the annual corporate planning process. Most major corporations gather their department and division managers together once each year to document the coming year's corporate objectives and to discuss the strategic and operational options that are critical to reaching those targets. If the IT Asset Allocation Analysis is run once a month for each division (as in Case Study 2), and corporate objectives are defined, then linking the two to make the corporate enterprise a point of discussion during the planning process would simply be a matter of presentation.

One means of presenting this information during the planning process is to commandeer a wall. At the top of the wall, in banner form, is a list of the summarized corporate objectives. Beneath this banner of objectives are the six bimonthly reports sorted by date and division. The effectiveness of this presentation is best conveyed via the illustration on the following page.

CORPORATE OBJECTIVES

Revenue Growth, Profits, Cost Containment, Acquisitions,
ROI, ROA, Downsizing, Reorganization, Expansion, etc.

(DIVISION TRENDS)

DIVISION 1 IT ASSET ANALYSIS	DIVISION 2 IT ASSET ANALYSIS	DIVISION 3 IT ASSET ANALYSIS	DIVISION 4 IT ASSET ANALYSIS	DIVISION 5 IT ASSET ANALYSIS	SEPT. (NOW)

(TIME-BASED ENTERPRISE VIEW)

DIVISION 1 IT ASSET ANALYSIS	DIVISION 2 IT ASSET ANALYSIS	DIVISION 3 IT ASSET ANALYSIS	DIVISION 4 IT ASSET ANALYSIS	DIVISION 5 IT ASSET ANALYSIS	JULY
DIVISION 1 IT ASSET ANALYSIS	DIVISION 2 IT ASSET ANALYSIS	DIVISION 3 IT ASSET ANALYSIS	DIVISION 4 IT ASSET ANALYSIS	DIVISION 5 IT ASSET ANALYSIS	MAY
DIVISION 1 IT ASSET ANALYSIS	DIVISION 2 IT ASSET ANALYSIS	DIVISION 3 IT ASSET ANALYSIS	DIVISION 4 IT ASSET ANALYSIS	DIVISION 5 IT ASSET ANALYSIS	MARCH
DIVISION 1 IT ASSET ANALYSIS	DIVISION 2 IT ASSET ANALYSIS	DIVISION 3 IT ASSET ANALYSIS	DIVISION 4 IT ASSET ANALYSIS	DIVISION 5 IT ASSET ANALYSIS	JAN.
DIVISION 1 IT ASSET ANALYSIS	DIVISION 2 IT ASSET ANALYSIS	DIVISION 3 IT ASSET ANALYSIS	DIVISION 4 IT ASSET ANALYSIS	DIVISION 5 IT ASSET ANALYSIS	NOV. (LAST YEAR)

Using this format, the division enterprises and the enterprise as a whole can be examined in light of the corporate mission. The vertical rows show the technology trend of a specific division, allowing you to determine if the current trend within a division is in harmony with the corporate objectives. The horizontal rows give you a picture of the corporate enterprise at a given moment in time, providing answers to questions such as, What did the enterprise look like when we did the reorganization last January?

A discussion of the IT Asset Allocation Analysis contained in Case Study 2, whether part of an annual plan or some other forum, is invaluable in focusing the distributed enterprise management team on the larger issues facing the corporate information technology base. This is by no means the only way to coordinate such an effort, but it is an easy and time-efficient medium that allows for a quantitative discussion of the issues.

CHAPTER 5

• POODLES AND DOBERMANS •

BEST OF BREED REQUIREMENTS

Me: I'm looking to buy a dog.

Dog Breeder: What kind of dog are you looking for?

Me: I'm looking for a smart, active, low-maintenance, easy-to-train, aggressive watchdog that is good with kids.

Dog Breeder: So am I, and if I find one, I plan to marry him.

As in my quest for a dog, perfection often involves contradiction. As the breeder would explain to me, "Smart dogs are often more difficult to train as they are distracted by all of the possibilities that surround them, aggressive dogs and children do not belong in the same sentence, and low-maintenance and active go together like oil and water." And so, in my quest for a dog some twenty-five years ago, I failed to describe a plausible dog, but achieved near perfection in describing the ideal functional qualities of an asset tracking system.

For those of you not fixated on dogs, let me translate these qualities into something you can identify with. An effective asset tracking system must be able to automatically translate its data into insightful analyses (smart). It must be able to accumulate and use multiple data points for each item it tracks (active). It should be a silent servant, not imposing any administrative burden on its owner (low maintenance). As it is impossible to anticipate all of the ways an asset tracking system can be used, it must provide easily accessible, ad hoc reporting (easy to train). It should actively audit the enterprise, searching for conditions that you deem to be harmful or questionable (aggressive watchdog). And most important, it must be transparent to the end users and server administrators (good with kids).

I have taken the time to define each of the above points in greater detail. Some of the topics will become more lucid as you review the case studies. But before flipping to the case studies, I encourage you to read this chapter as it gives you a look at the whole dog—and the possibilities that exist in a properly designed system.

ANALYSIS (SMART)

Analysis is the art of seeing the steps to a conclusion and logically presenting the information required in a format that facilitates a decision. Analysis does not focus on the specific, but rather defines the field of play. Regardless of the size of your enterprise or the nature of your business, there are specific analyses that apply to common functions within each organization. For example, the operations department needs to know the true cost and end-user impact of upgrading an application. Finance needs analyses comparing the asset base over different time periods. Purchasing needs vendor trend analyses. And legal demands license compliance analyses. Each of these analyses requires progressive steps of gathering data, and through organized methods, turning that data into information.

For example, if you want to compute the cost of upgrading the finance department to the latest version of a spreadsheet, you would ultimately need to go through the following process:

1) Ascertain the number of desktops in finance.

2) Determine how many desktops use the spreadsheet.

3) Determine if any of them already have the proposed upgrade.

4) Determine the prerequisites (CPU speed, memory, free disk space, operating system revision) for the new revision of the spreadsheet.

5) Apply the prerequisites against the end users who require the new spreadsheet version in order to determine which users need system upgrades as part of their spreadsheet upgrade.

6) Once the required quantity of upgrade components (CPU speed, memory, free disk space, operating system revision) is known, research the cost for each of the upgrade components, including the spreadsheet upgrade. Note: Knowing the quantities of the components required allows you to spend the majority of your time scrubbing the costs of components that have the greatest impact on the total cost of the upgrade.

7) Isolate (compute by cost type) the various cost components to determine if further research is warranted and to ascertain the operational feasibility of the upgrade.

8) Ascertain the impact of such an upgrade on user productivity (downtime in implementing the upgrade), as well as the IT resources required to implement the proposed change.

9) Solicit the additional specific information required to facilitate the upgrade or justify canceling the program.

The above nine steps show how an analysis is executed, one step at a time. If your asset tracking system had a comprehensive set of analyses, you could accomplish all of the above in a two-step process:

1) Identify the department, its package prerequisites, and their estimated costs.

2) Print or display the analysis.

Ideally, this system-generated analysis should present its findings in a manner that follows the human thought process. It should make optimum use of text, tables, and graphs to facilitate a decision. For an example of a system-generated analysis, see the case study at the end of this chapter.

SAMPLING OF DATA POINTS (ACTIVE)

An asset inventory tells you what your distributed enterprise looks like at a given moment in time. An asset tracking system tells you the current state of the enterprise, where it has been, and the direction in which it is evolving. This is accomplished through the capture and maintenance of multiple snapshots of the asset base over time, allowing for both a regression and sensitivity analysis of the distributed enterprise. These analyses can be focused at the desktop level, enterprise level, or any level in between.

Without this time-based gathering of asset information, much of what has been discussed in earlier chapters (Time Comparative Anchors, Trends Comparative Anchors, Null Comparative Anchors, corporate security examples, purchasing examples, etc.), would not be possible. Having an active asset tracking system that accumulates snapshots of individual items over time allows you to gain insight in three ways:

• It allows you to view all or part of your network at a given moment in time and compare it to some event external to the asset tracking system. What type of desktop (processor type) was the branch banking software originally deployed on? How many new servers did we install in Europe last year? Who was the last person to install XYZ application? These are examples of questions that link time and an external event or structure.

• It allows you to compare multiple snapshots of the same item and develop a trend or comparison. What is the growth rate of word processor X? What is the growth rate in end-user hard disk storage over the past six quarters? Which desktops are reporting a decline in main memory since the last snapshot? These are the types of questions that draw on historical trends within individual items.

- It allows you to draw comparisons between different items during the same or different time periods, creating new insights. How has the distribution of word processor applications across job classifications changed over the past two years? Over the past three years, what is the frequency of main memory upgrades for users who today have three or more Microsoft products? The possibilities for combining data items into meaningful insights is infinite.

Once the power of having historical snapshots of individual items is understood, the question arises as to how often snapshots (inventories of the desktops and servers associated with a specific date) should be taken. This decision will be influenced by several factors:

- How difficult is it to take a snapshot of the enterprise? Asset tracking systems that place a heavy administrative burden on the IT resources are labor intensive. Asset tracking systems that require end-user involvement will, out of necessity, restrict the frequency of snapshots.

- How heavy is the network load? Asset tracking systems that use the network to gather snapshots will necessarily put an additional burden on the network. This traffic can be minimized by batching these snapshots at the server level and then sending them to a central repository. Using non-peak hours can also minimize network strains. If using non-peak hours is a consideration, you should avoid using asset tracking systems that send snapshots as part of a startup sequence because most networks are under heavy use during startup hours.

- For many organizations, the ideal snapshot frequency is implemented around a "revolving schedule." A revolving schedule takes snapshots of some percentage of the enterprise on a regular schedule, completing a full-enterprise inventory over a desirable interval. For example, if a company optimally wanted weekly snapshots of the enterprise, but because of network constraints a full-enterprise inventory was only feasible once a month, a revolving schedule may be the answer. Using a revolving schedule, snapshots would be taken of one-seventh of the enterprise each night. This would distribute network load and allow for a weekly update of the enterprise. A perceived drawback of this methodology is that the enterprise is not captured in unison at a given moment in time. This is true, but in most cases the value of having more frequent updates far outweighs the lack of perfect synchronization.

The value of end-user time is a major consideration in determining the frequency of snapshots. With few exceptions, the greater the concern for end-user productivity, the more frequent the snapshots. This observation is tied to improving help desk response, to reacting quickly to upgrades and enhancements to the enterprise, and to being responsive to the business needs of the functional organizations.

Often, a critical reporting requirement will dictate the snapshot schedule. For example, an insurance company may need to verify the state of all desktops that are involved in policy writing once each week.

ADMINISTRATION
(LOW MAINTENANCE)

An asset tracking system should not create additional burdens in managing the enterprise. Specifically, it should be easy to install at all levels. This includes the central repository, servers, and desktops. This one-time installation may seem like a small consideration, but depending on the architecture of the system selected, the implementation costs can be ten times the cost of the asset tracking system!

One of the best ways to avoid surprises in this area is to purchase a two-server, 100-client version of the proposed system and install it prior to committing to a full-enterprise implementation. This is cheap insurance, as the experience gained in this limited installation may lead you to reconsider the system you selected and/or the means of deployment. For more information on implementation issues, see chapter 13.

Ideally, administration of the enterprise asset repository should be a "lights-out" operation. No human intervention should be required when a new desktop is reported to the repository or when a new item (element) is discovered on a desktop or server. With the exception of telling the system you want it to begin tracking a new element of information, the system should gather its information on a predetermined schedule, totally unattended.

EASILY ACCESSIBLE, AD HOC REPORTING (EASY TO TRAIN)

As mentioned earlier, it is impossible to predict all of the uses for an enterprise-wide IT asset tracking system. Within this uncertainty, however, there is vast opportunity. As psychologist Erich Fromm said in *Man For Himself,* "The quest for certainty blocks the search for meaning. Uncertainty is the very condition to impel man to unfold his powers." If the full power of an enterprise asset tracking system is to be "unfolded," the raw information in the repository must be accessible at three levels:

TO THE IT TECHNICAL PROFESSIONAL

This professional, through writing code or using specialized data extraction tools (e.g., structured query language [SQL] tools), should have infinite flexibility in manipulating the repository. This ability is key as each organization and enterprise is unique, and there is no system or solution that can anticipate all of the value to be derived from the captured information.

With this flexibility, consideration must be given to the human resources that manage the enterprise. To effectively leverage the IT technical professional, the information within the repository should be well documented and easily accessible.

To Non-technical Management

The system should provide an interface to tool sets that enable managers to easily extract information that is relevant to their responsibilities. In chapter 4, we saw how the purchasing, finance, corporate security, help desk, operations, general management, and legal departments could make valuable use of an asset tracking repository. Some of the information these department managers need may only be met with the assistance of an IT technical professional; however, with an easy user interface, these managers can directly access the repository and gain insights that allow them to quickly make informed decisions.

User tools in this area include easy-to-use report writers, canned reports that allow users to change predefined variables, and the ability to export information directly into a "user-enabled environment" such as a spreadsheet.

To Other Applications

An effective implementation of an asset tracking solution allows other management tools and applications to extend their functionality. Assuming the proper architecture, the asset repository can easily export information or provide a "live link" to other operations. This topic is covered in greater detail in chapter 6.

ACTIVELY AUDIT THE ENTERPRISE
(AGGRESSIVE WATCHDOG)

Every good asset tracking system should come with its own auditor. Once the asset tracking system is installed, the auditor—green eyeshade, armbands and all—should somehow be digitized and injected into the enterprise. This auditor should do what all auditors do: use his or her training and experience to monitor and report dangerous, or potentially dangerous, situations. Without the technology to digitize a human auditor, the next best option is to use our knowledge of what is dangerous, or potentially dangerous, to the enterprise, along with the "legs" of an asset tracking system, to create an electronic auditor. The auditing function should be viewed as a major and necessary component of any asset tracking system.

This electronic auditing function should allow you to easily define conditions you want audited and then, either automatically or upon request, conduct an audit that reports on those desktops and servers that fail to meet the audit criteria. There is an unlimited number of uses for the audit function, but most fall into one of four categories:

Enforcement of Standards

The most obvious use of the auditor is the enforcement of desktop standards. The advantage to having an asset tracking system do the audit is that it can tell you not only when a system falls out of standards, but it can also tell you specifically how it fails to meet desired criteria.

Targeted Business Requirements

You may wish to be informed whenever a file server exceeds 85 percent capacity. A business unit manager may have a productivity problem and wish to be informed when users have games installed on their systems. Any targeted item, or combination of items, can become part of an audit.

PREVENTIVE MEASURES

As you discover problems within the enterprise (via the help desk, business managers, or suppliers), you can have the auditor monitor the enterprise and report new occurrences of the condition. This allows those operating the enterprise to be proactive and disarm problems before they manifest.

EDUCATE THE USER BASE

Another powerful use of an auditor is education. For example, it was discovered that the latest version (Version 3.25) of an operating system is incompatible with Spreadsheet Inc.'s Version 6. With an auditor, every current and future user of Version 6 spreadsheet could be warned not to upgrade their operating system to Version 3.25. We read about dozens of alerts from software vendors each week; the auditor gives you the ability to apply this knowledge to the enterprise.

TRANSPARENT TO THE END USER AND SERVER ADMINISTRATOR (GOOD WITH KIDS)

With a single exception, the asset tracking system should be transparent to end users and server administrators. The exception should be a facility allowing the end user or administrator to take a snapshot on demand. This on-demand snapshot allows the end user or server administrator to send the help desk professional an up-to-the-minute snapshot of the problem desktop or server.

SUMMARY

An effective "system" is nothing more than a feedback loop, providing effortless answers and insights into the questions it generates.

CASE STUDY 3
THE DRIBBLE EFFECT

PROLOGUE

Mega Bank is a large bank that has an active acquisition strategy. It averages one large merger/acquisition each year and one small acquisition each quarter. Mega Bank's business model calls for a distributed enterprise that is managed via a corporate MIS function. There is a hierarchical MIS structure that has dotted-line reporting to the various business unit executives. The design and management of the distributed enterprise falls under the senior vice president of information resources, with funding sign-off required by the individual business units. Major modifications to the structure of the enterprise and/or substantial changes to the quality of delivered services are managed at the senior vice president level via the quarterly and annual planning processes.

ENTERPRISE DEFINITION

Mega Bank's distributed enterprise consists of 60,000 desktops, supported by 3,600 servers. The largest concentration of desktops and servers (46 percent) is installed in the greater New York City area. The three major division headquarters locations represent 24 percent of the distributed enterprise, branch operations 20 percent, and international operations 10 percent.

Due to its merger/acquisition strategy over the past three years, Mega Bank has experienced a 27 percent compound annual growth rate in the number of servers and desktops supported as part of the distributed enterprise. In addition, although migrating toward a standard server and workstation paradigm, Mega Bank has been required to expand its enterprise definition to support two new server platforms and three new desktop platforms.

The Situation/Problem

Mega Bank's successful expansion program has had the undesirable effect of increasing the unplanned annual desktop and server expenditures from $90 per desktop to $207 per desktop. The majority of this 230 percent increase (from $5.4 million to $12.4 million) in unbudgeted expenses falls into five upgrade categories: software, memory, CPU (processor), hard disk (online storage), and operating system.

A cursory review has determined that the primary source of unplanned spending is the upgrading of application software to a new revision. These upgrades often have prerequisites that exceed the recommended individual desktop configurations and require the user to request additional memory, hard disk storage, operating system software, or processing capacity in order to effectively run the new version of the application software.

Action Plan

Having recently installed a comprehensive asset tracking system, the senior vice president of information resources directs that all future software upgrades involving more than 100 desktops have a "full-cost model" of the upgrade prepared prior to the upgrade decision. On the third of October, the first proposed upgrade to fall under this policy is received from the finance department. The purchase order requisition calls for upgrading 2,229 copies of Spreadsheet Inc.'s spreadsheet application to Version 6.0 for $111,450 ($50 per copy). The analysis, which ultimately does not support this request, is detailed below.

The Analysis

As in the previous case studies, it is important that the provided analysis be easily "digested" and presented on a single page. In this Software Upgrade Analysis, having the information on a single page affords the reader two advantages. First, it allows the reader to view the relationship between the various elements of the report. And second, it allows the reader to quickly scan a large number of upgrade requests and focus attention only on those that have the greatest impact.

A nearly ideal Software Upgrade Analysis is diagrammed on the following pages. There are five sections to this report, each providing its own insight into the proposed upgrade. *Note: Although such a report would ideally appear on a single page, this chapter presents the sections in a series.*

Before beginning the Software Upgrade Analysis, the asset tracking system needs some information about the proposed upgrade. This information is summarized in the fourth section of the analysis (see the illustration on the following page entitled Change Analysis), but is included here, out of order, as a means of summarizing the input prompted by the asset tracking system as part of the analysis preparation.

CHANGE ANALYSIS

DEPARTMENT - **FINANCE**
APPLICATION- **SPREADSHEET 6.0**
DESCRIPTION : ANALYSIS OF THE RESOURCES REQUIRED TO
UPGRADE THE FINANCE DEPARTMENT TO SPREADSHEET 6.0.

PREREQUISITES

MEMORY - **8192K**
CPU - **486**
FREE DISK - **16MB**
SOFTWARE - **SPREADSHEET 1.0**
O.S. - **WIN 95**

COST DATA

UPGRADE TO SPREADSHEET 6.0 - **$50**
OPERATING SYSTEM UPGRADE - **$75**
MEMORY UPGRADE - **$200**
MEMORY UPGRADE UNIT - **8MB**
DISK UPGRADE - **$200**
DISK UPGRADE UNIT - **600MB**
CPU UPGRADE - **$1,200**
LABOR - **$95/HR**
LOST PRODUCTIVITY - **$105/HR**

TIME REQUIRED (HOURS)

SPREADSHEET 6.0 - **3**
OPERATING SYSTEM UPGRADE - **5**
MEMORY UPGRADE - **2**
DISK UPGRADE - **4**
CPU UPGRADE - **6**

The information highlighted in bold type was entered by the person running the analysis. Ideally, the person running the analysis should be able to either directly enter the prompted value or select the value from a list provided by the asset tracking system. Once this information has been entered, the analysis is generated.

SOFTWARE UPGRADE ANALYSIS

SOFTWARE UPGRADE ANALYSIS – SUMMARY

The first section of this analysis, the Summary, provides an overview of the proposed upgrade.

SUMMARY

There are 2,229 desktops (workstations and servers) in the Finance Department. Of these, 29 already have Version 6.0 installed, and 80 do not meet the specified eligibility requirements. No costs are calculated for these desktops. Of the remaining 2,120 eligible desktops, 1,420 meet the specified prerequisites, and only require the new software version at a cost of $71,000. Additionally, upgrading these 1,420 desktops will result in a direct labor cost of $404,700 and a lost productivity cost of $447,300. The other 700 eligible desktops fail to meet at least one prerequisite and require an operating system and/or hardware upgrade in addition to the new software version, at a cost of $680,025. Additionally, upgrading these 700 desktops will result in a direct labor cost of $689,225 and a lost productivity cost of $761,775. The total cost of implementing this upgrade is $3,054,025.

The person responsible for analyzing the request to upgrade the spreadsheet application in the finance department need only look at the purchase requisition for $111,450 and the last number in the Summary, $3,054,025, to determine the need for further consideration. In this case, the Summary indicates that the actual cost of upgrading finance to be more than twenty-seven times higher than the requested amount.

Having determined a wide variance between the proposed cost and the estimated cost, an examination of the other sections of the analysis is warranted.

Software Upgrade Analysis – Desktop Distribution

The second section of the analysis (see illustration entitled Desktop Distribution) provides a high-level breakdown of the upgrade across the desktops. This is especially useful to those who are responsible for installing and supporting the upgraded systems. Desktops that demand a hardware and/or operating system modification as part of an application upgrade usually require a disproportionate amount of support resources. This knowledge can be invaluable in planning for the implementation and help desk resources required to support the proposed application upgrade. The following chart quickly tells those responsible for supporting the enterprise that a significant portion, 700, of the users upgrading this application will require substantial technical support services.

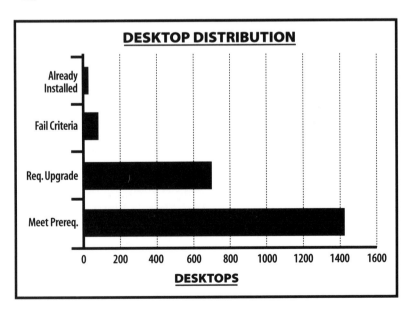

Support resources and the cost of materials only tell part of the story for these 700 desktops that need to be modified before receiving the Spreadsheet 6.0 upgrade. The associated impact on user productivity, as illustrated in Section 3, Cost Breakdown, may be the most significant factor in determining the feasibility and methodology of an application upgrade.

Software Upgrade Analysis – Cost Breakdown

Section 1 and Section 2 provide a high-level understanding of the cost and support requirements for the proposed upgrade. Section 3 presents a cross section of detail summarizing the proposed upgrade, both by expense components and type of expense. It is in this section that the impact of labor expenses and the cost of lost productivity are introduced. These numbers are calculated from the entered values as summarized in Section 4, Change Analysis.

Before examining the results in Section 3, there are two columns of information, "Labor" and "Lost Productivity," that deserve special consideration because they represent items that are often overlooked when calculating the cost of an application upgrade. The "Labor" column includes the salary expense (i.e., the fully loaded labor rate) of the IT professionals supporting the effort. The "Lost Productivity" column includes the labor expense for the end user, plus some lost opportunity tied to how much product or revenue the employee will be unable to produce as a result of not having access to the desktop. For example, a telesales person who is separated from the desktop for two hours may have a fully loaded cost to the company of $200, but during that same two hours have the ability to generate $1,000 of revenue/orders. In this example, I have kept the hourly rate at an extremely conservative $105 in order to show that even a low number can have a profound impact.

As the following chart illustrates, "Labor" and "Lost Productivity" substantially exceed the cost of purchasing the required hardware and software. The two columns represent nearly half of the projected cost of the undertaking. Further, the total in the "Materials" column highlights the cost of implementing the 700 users who do not meet the hardware and software prerequisites of the proposed spreadsheet upgrade. Here we discover the reason that the $680,025 material cost of the upgrade is more than six times the original budget estimate of $111,450.

COST BREAKDOWN FOR THE 700 DESKTOPS FAILING PREREQUISITES					
ITEM	UNIT	MATERIALS	LABOR	LOST PRODUCTIVITY	TOTAL
MEMORY	580	$116,000	$110,200	$121,800	$348,000
CPU	396	$475,200	$225,720	$249,480	$950,400
SOFTWARE	700	$35,000	$199,500	$220,500	$455,000
HARD DISKS	211	$42,200	$80,180	$88,620	$211,000
OS	155	$11,625	$73,625	$81,375	$166,625
TOTAL	N/A	$680,025	$689,225	$761,775	$2,131,025

After reviewing the results of the Cost Breakdown, most individuals are shocked at the projected cost of the upgrade. It is for this reason that an effective analysis provides the manager with a review of the values that were the basis of the analysis. Here, if errors were made, they can be corrected and the analysis rerun to reflect those corrections.

Software Upgrade Analysis — Change Analysis
(Duplicate)

CHANGE ANALYSIS

DEPARTMENT - **FINANCE**
APPLICATION - **SPREADSHEET 6.0**
DESCRIPTION : ANALYSIS OF THE RESOURCES REQUIRED TO
UPGRADE THE FINANCE DEPARTMENT TO SPREADSHEET 6.0.

PREREQUISITES

MEMORY - **8192K**
CPU - **486**
FREE DISK - **16MB**
SOFTWARE - **SPREADSHEET 1.0**
O.S. - **WIN 95**

COST DATA

UPGRADE TO SPREADSHEET 6.0 - **$50**
OPERATING SYSTEM UPGRADE - **$75**
MEMORY UPGRADE - **$200**
MEMORY UPGRADE UNIT - **8MB**
DISK UPGRADE - **$200**
DISK UPGRADE UNIT - **600MB**
CPU UPGRADE - **$1,200**
LABOR - **$95/HR**
LOST PRODUCTIVITY - **$105/HR**

TIME REQUIRED (HOURS)

SPREADSHEET 6.0 - **3**
OPERATING SYSTEM UPGRADE - **5**
MEMORY UPGRADE - **2**
DISK UPGRADE - **4**
CPU UPGRADE - **6**

In revisiting Section 4, we can now focus on those areas that have the greatest cost impact on the project. In this case, special attention would be given to the CPU and memory costs because they represent the largest unplanned expense items.

Software Upgrade Analysis – Expense Distribution

Section 5 highlights the expense distribution (excluding labor and lost productivity costs) of the upgrade. The pie chart graphically compares each cost component to the total projected expense.

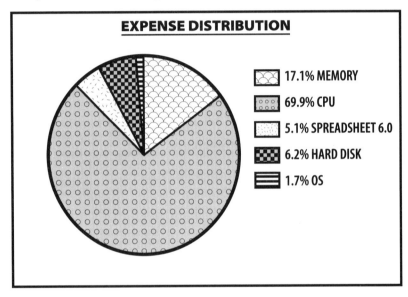

Section 5 immediately highlights the fact that the Spreadsheet 6.0 application portion of the proposed upgrade is only 5.1 percent of the total cost of upgrading the spreadsheet software on finance's desktops. In fact, from a cost perspective, based on the variables provided and documented in Section 4, this upgrade has more to do with upgrading the central processing units than all other factors.

It is when examining these relationships that Sections 4 and 5 work together. Having an automated analysis allows those entering the variables to minimize the time they spend researching the cost of the various upgrade components. In this example, the person entered an operating system upgrade cost of $75 and a CPU-upgrade cost of $1,200. These were rough estimates and fall within a rational sampling of market prices.

Both of these cost items, however, are highly configuration dependent. The true cost of upgrading either the operating system or the CPU hinges on the specific workstation starting and ending point. Clearly, an in-depth analysis of each cost component and the computation of a precise average cost for each item is possible. The luxury of having an asset tracking system should, however, save you extensive research on the cost of each component.

Consider the following questions that can be answered with just the rough approximations that were entered. With an estimated materials and labor expense of more than $1.8 million and a total cost, including lost productivity, of more than $3 million, does it make sense to give this upgrade further consideration? Based on the cost distribution, does it make sense to spend time fine-tuning any of the cost values other than the cost of upgrading the application and processor? Considering the cost of this upgrade, is there a more cost-effective way to meet the users' needs that does not involve Spreadsheet 6.0? What if you found a way to cut the cost of CPU upgrades by 40 percent? Would any of the answers to the above questions change?

By comparing and contrasting the information contained in Sections 4 and 5, iterative analyses can be run, establishing "sensitivity parameters" that can help avoid costly research efforts. In addition, the same reports can be of substantial value in justifying a decision to those making the request for expenditures.

Epilogue

An epilogue is included in this hypothetical case study to highlight some of the discoveries that MIS professionals have shared with me in the management of their distributed enterprise.

The above analysis resulted in the following actions and decisions:

• Given the timing of the downtime and considerable disruption (identified while calculating the above support effort) to the 700 users who require component upgrades, the finance department decided to postpone the Spreadsheet upgrade for now. Regardless of cost, any such disruption would have to be scheduled for the early summer months.

• The original reason for requesting the upgrade was centered on compatibility issues. As a result, users experiencing compatibility issues were upgraded to Spreadsheet 4.5, which did not require extensive hardware upgrades.

• As a result of this exercise, an IT Asset Analysis (see Case Study 2) for the finance department was run. This analysis revealed the need for a scheduled technology upgrade that would include some form of spreadsheet standardization. This upgrade was scheduled for the summer months.

From Theory to Application

This case study highlights the utility of the analysis portion of an asset tracking system. It would seem to ignore the other critical components of asset tracking, such as maintaining historical snapshots, the audit function, ad hoc reporting, and end-user transparency. In the real world, however, much of what was discussed in this case study would require all components outlined in this chapter in order to realize all benefits outlined in the case study.

Specifically, many of the targeted questions that are raised as a result of running the analysis in Case Study 3 would be answered via an ad hoc query/reporting system. If this system fails to make the asset repository accessible to all levels of those using the analyses, then the analyses will do nothing more than generate an ever-growing number of unanswered questions.

Maintaining multiple snapshots (history) of each workstation and server allows those planning the future, via historical trends, to anticipate future requirements. In this case study, how valuable would it be to know that the rest of the corporation is moving away from the Spreadsheet Inc. product, or that the finance department is slowly migrating toward an operating system or application that is incompatible with Spreadsheet 6.0?

Once a stable spreadsheet platform is established in the finance department, it must be maintained or the investment in stability is lost. An automated audit function could be set up to catch any configuration or application anomalies that might affect the compatibility or performance of the selected spreadsheet application.

These examples, and more, are successful extensions of the single analysis highlighted in Case Study 3 with each component supporting and adding value to the other. And supporting all of this functionality is the critical ease-of-use and ease-of-administration issue. If the asset tracking system is to be effective, it must not burden the user or the administrator. For every unit of complexity that is added to a broad-based information resource, such as an asset tracking system, three units of utility are lost. It is not complexity that makes a system powerful, but utility and application.

CHAPTER 6

• UTENSILS AND ROMANCE •
EMPOWERING OTHER ASSETS

Me: *(After traveling more than an hour without seeing another living soul)* Where are we?

Beautiful Companion: We, Mr. "Type A" business executive, are at the world's most perfect picnic spot! See, we have the requisite grove of walnut trees, the babbling brook, a grassy bank for the picnic blanket, and a sunny seventy-eight degrees!

Me: *(After setting up the picnic site)* And what do we have for lunch?

Beautiful Companion: Fresh-baked French bread, a warm wheel of Brie cheese, crisp sliced apples, cold boneless Cornish hens with cranberry glaze, and…a very expensive bottle of your favorite Chardonnay.

Me: You mean…

Beautiful Companion: *(Holding up the bottle)* That's right, your favorite vintage.

Me: Let the picnic begin! Hand me the corkscrew.

Beautiful Companion: Corkscrew?

To be honest, it still turned out to be a wonderful picnic; but it would have been even better if we had celebrated with that exquisite bottle of wine. The wine in this case was a catalyst, having the ability to raise the value of everything it touched. Now, I would not put an asset tracking system in the same league as a near-perfect bottle of Chardonnay, but it does share the Chardonnay's ability to make associated assets more valuable.

There is a wide range of enterprise assets that have the potential not only to gain value, but to multiply value as a result of having access to an asset tracking system. A partial list of these assets that benefit from the value multiplier include: help desk systems, capacity planning tools, software distribution tools, network planning tools, change management tools, business applications, fixed-asset accounting systems, and facilities planning and maintenance systems.

The remainder of this chapter is devoted to a brief discussion of how asset tracking can further empower these applications, and it defines the qualities that an asset tracking system must have to make such empowerment possible.

EMPOWERING ASSETS

HELP DESK SYSTEMS

Since several examples have already shown how an asset tracking system can add value to a help desk service, I will forego the utility portion of this discussion. Mechanically, however, there is a great opportunity to improve productivity of the help desk application, the help desk professional, and the end user if the asset tracking system can be integrated into the help desk application. By extracting a subset of the asset tracking information and loading it into the relevant data structures of the help desk application, the analysis and tracking functions of the help desk application can include a detailed knowledge of the asset that is in question.

In reverse, it may be desirable to load portions of the help desk system into the asset tracking repository (assuming your help desk application has an export facility). With this information in the asset tracking system, you would be able to ask questions about your distributed asset base and relate them to the number or types of problems.

CAPACITY PLANNING TOOLS

Those who are involved in capacity planning have the responsibility to plan both the quantitative and qualitative aspects of the future enterprise.

Quantitatively, an asset tracking system can pass raw numbers concerning the past and current structures of the enterprise to the modeling tools used by capacity planners. Providing the capacity planning function with a current and historical analysis of the desktop and server enterprise will allow for a more accurate forecast. Qualitatively, an asset tracking system can provide capacity planning models with information such as which applications are running on which machines, or what servers have access to the sales department database. For example, it may be very important to know that 50 percent of workstations and servers in finance use the sales database.

CHARGE-BACK SYSTEMS

Because the management and support of a distributed IT enterprise is both complex and expensive, IT executives have instituted charge-back systems with the objective of tying support costs to those resources consuming support services. At the same time, end-user empowerment and the accelerating rate of change across the desktop/server enterprise have inhibited the ability to forecast and associate expenses with specific configurations and applications.

An asset tracking system that integrates with an automated charge-back system has the ability to assign a specific support cost to each desktop asset, and produce a charge-back allocation that accurately reflects the cost of supporting an individual configuration. With this capability, those managing the enterprise have the ability to "economically lead" the enterprise of users toward configurations that are cost-effective to maintain and support.

With the integration of an asset tracking system and a charge-back system in place, those making a selection of hardware, software, or combinations thereof would know that their decisions will automatically be reported to the charge-back system, and that they will be billed accordingly. This integration provides a powerful financial incentive for user departments to move toward a desired standard of maintainable configurations.

SOFTWARE DISTRIBUTION TOOLS

Part of managing the enterprise is coordinating numerous changes to distributed applications. Distributing new applications, new revisions of applications, and the coordinated distribution and collection of valuable business information in many instances are configuration dependent. By empowering an electronic software distribution system with access to an asset tracking system, you can target distributions for specific users based on their desktop configurations. In addition, a distribution can be modeled before being deployed. This modeling allows you to correct any inconsistencies between the distribution and the configuration, allowing for corrective action to be taken prior to deployment.

The link between an asset tracking system and a software distribution system has the potential to greatly reduce the time consumed by both the help desk professional and end user in correcting failed distributions. This link also makes it feasible to leverage the benefits of electronic distributions over a larger portion of the heterogeneous enterprise.

NETWORK MANAGEMENT TOOLS

A communications line goes down. As a result, your network management tool sends out alerts, begins automated recovery procedures, reports that it cannot correct the problem, and publishes a suite of network addresses that are unavailable to the enterprise. The network management staff is now charged with the task of ascertaining the problem, finding a solution, and determining the impact on business. By keeping a subset of the asset tracking repository loaded into the network management system database, or by maintaining a dynamic link between the two systems, the network management professionals, in addition to receiving network addresses, would be provided with end-user names, titles, department designations, phone numbers, critical applications that run on each affected address, and critical configuration information. With this information, the network management professionals can better establish priorities and gain insight into the impact the failure will have on business operations.

OPERATIONS CHANGE MANAGEMENT SYSTEMS

In most large enterprises, there is a group that manages changes to business operations. These individuals are responsible for evaluating and planning the movement of departments from one physical location to another, the redeployment of space, and all facets of logistics that involve physical changes. There are a number of powerful automated tools available to assist in this area. These tools track the logistics and interdependencies of all actions associated with change.

Exceptional benefits can be realized by integrating the asset repository with these change control systems. With the integration of the two systems, the change control software will be able to identify all the affected, networked users by their departments, specific physical location, and how they are attached to the network. The configuration and associated electrical power requirements can also be made available to the change system. A more detailed discussion of change will be provided in chapter 12.

BUSINESS APPLICATIONS

The value of integrating an asset tracking system with business applications is dependent on the nature and structure of the business. Because a robust asset tracking system can query the end user or server administrator for information, and because the snapshots of the desktops or servers can contain non-IT information, there are infinite integration possibilities. This type of integration is less common than the types of integration listed above; however, when implemented, business integration typically offers the greatest return on investment.

FIXED-ASSET ACCOUNTING SYSTEMS

One of the most difficult tasks facing financial professionals is accounting for the distributed IT assets. The two traditional means of building a knowledge base of IT assets are: 1) a physical inventory, and 2) reconstruction of the enterprise from purchasing records. Both methods are often used by the finance department to create an accounting of the IT assets within the fixed-asset accounting system.

There are many reasons why fixed-asset accounting systems fail to accurately reflect the enterprise. These include: distributed buying authority, cannibalization of systems, unknown retirement of desktops and servers, migration of technology within and among departments, theft, and upgrades. All of these elements, and more, keep even the most diligent asset manager guessing as to the true value, type, and quantity of the assets that make up the distributed enterprise.

Linking the asset tracking repository to the fixed-asset accounting system allows for a comparison of assets by identification number, asset description, department, etc. Automated matching of the asset detail within the two systems enables the responsible party to focus on the exceptions. Clearly, the first efforts in this area will result in as many exceptions as matches; however, over time the systems will synchronize, allowing for meaningful exception handling.

Another option for solving the reconciliation issue is to use the asset tracking system as the source for the financial tracking of the IT asset base. This would require a one-time reconciliation to bring the databases into harmony; but once reconciled, the asset tracking system could automatically update the fixed-asset system as often as desired. Such an implementation is attractive because it eliminates the expense of a complete physical audit; it eliminates the reconciliation headaches encountered when assets are inventoried over a period of time; and it provides a more accurate snapshot of the distributed IT asset base.

QUALITIES REQUIRED TO EMPOWER OTHER APPLICATIONS

In writing this book, I promised myself to limit my discussion of technology to a single chapter. As this is not the chapter, I will endeavor to tie each of the empowerment (technical) attributes back to its practical application. Technical or not, the following four attributes enable an asset tracking system to reach beyond its intended purpose and extend the utility of other mission-critical functions.

HEARING FROM THE END USER

In almost all of the previous examples, there are items that cannot be discovered electronically. For example, even the best asset tracking system cannot read the asset identification sticker on the side of a monitor. The same holds true for the end-user's mailing address or the fax number nearest his or her desk. Although this information cannot be discovered electronically, it can be gathered electronically. A full-featured asset tracking system has the ability to electronically send information requests to the end user and then associate the response with either the user, desktop, or any other attribute.

Other applications and tool sets often require information that cannot be read electronically. A business application may need to know the account numbers associated with the user's activity. A help desk application may need to store some form of billing code, etc. As you think through the process of empowering other applications, you will discover that without occasionally hearing from the end user, "It is difficult to get there from here."

THINGS CHANGE

No one has the ability to predict what information will be required in the future. In the case of asset empowerment, by improving the features of their products, vendors may indirectly influence what is required from the asset tracking system.

In other words, technology moves quickly. For example, several years ago it would have seemed preposterous to plan on every desktop having its own DVD-ROM; today, we see it as just a matter of time. This insight brings two requirements to the forefront. First, an asset tracking system must be able to extend the range of what it discovers; and second, in adding to its reach, it must not require a reinstallation of the tracking system on the desktops and servers. If the asset tracking system is to be a true enabler, it must painlessly extend the scope of its reach across the enterprise.

The same painless extension also applies to the administration of the repository. The addition of a new item to be tracked should not require any interaction with or administration of the asset repository. As the new asset information is received, the repository should dynamically create and link the new asset item with the associated assets.

INTEGRATION MADE EASY

In selecting application and tool vendors, the ability of the product to solve a problem is typically the primary buying criterion. Once the product is installed and is delivering the proposed benefit, it often becomes attractive to integrate it with other applications or business processes. Here the "vendor dance" begins. Each application/tool vendor lists the required criteria for interfacing with other applications. Then, the customer is left with the task of unraveling the file, record, and/or data structures in an attempt to create a conduit between the applications. This can be a time-consuming and expensive process, and it should come as no surprise that it generally involves the vendor's consulting group.

In the case of asset tracking systems, this process is especially burdensome because of the broad utility of the asset tracking repository. The solution is not to double your consulting budget, but to place the "data request" and/or "data delivery" burden on the asset tracking system.

REACHING THE UNREACHABLE
(THOSE NOT PART OF THE NETWORK)

When we speak of networked users, we typically include users who have a physical connection to the enterprise. There is, however, another class of users who are networked in a different manner. These users make up the business network and are often included in the scope of applications that an asset tracking system can empower. They include physically connected users, users who enter the enterprise through a public data network, and users who have no electronic connection to the enterprise.

Within the business network, users share a common mission, are part of the same organization, and/or supply a valuable service to the organization. Mobile sales professionals, suppliers, customers, and contract workers are some of the resources that may have no direct physical connection to the enterprise, but have a direct connection to the business network.

If this group of users is to be brought under the asset tracking umbrella, several extensions to traditional asset tracking methodology must be employed. First, the desktop must use an auto-inventory methodology; that is to say, the desktop must be able to inventory itself. Once this auto-inventory is complete, the asset tracking system should provide a number of methods for gathering the snapshots of the desktops and servers not connected to the physical enterprise. These methods include: automatic capture when the user accesses the Internet through a company gateway, an end-user submitted diskette, and remote server capture and transmission.

The technical details of how these capture methods work is not as important as making certain that the selected asset tracking system has the ability to capture snapshots of all users in the business enterprise. Of primary concern when considering a capture method is the routine of the end user. The more natural the collection method is to the routine of the end user, the higher the success rate will be in capturing the asset snapshots.

SUMMARY

There is no greater calling than that of making others better, for in standing near their greatness we are illuminated in their light.

CASE STUDY 4
NOW YOU KNOW

PROLOGUE

Case studies in previous chapters have centered on hypothetical organizations and their specific problems. For reasons that will be expanded upon in a moment, this case study focuses on a generic problem that is at the heart of managing every distributed enterprise—knowing what assets you have.

Whether you are a Fortune 100 manufacturer, a regional bank, an insurance carrier, a government agency, or a retail provider, you share a common challenge in managing the distributed enterprise. You are faced with the legal responsibility and business necessity of knowing the quantities and attributes of items that comprise your distributed enterprise. The question is so simple: What do we have out there? Yet for a complexity of reasons, control and knowledge of this asset base (which is often valued at hundreds of millions of dollars) is elusive, time consuming, and expensive.

ENTERPRISE DEFINITION

It would be unfair to say that all aspects of the enterprise are unmanaged. Those parts that are under the control of a single entity, such as MIS, are often some of the most accounted for assets. For example, the network of bridges and routers often falls under the dominion of a single individual or department. Here, the ordering, upgrading, and management of these resources can be tracked and controlled efficiently. Similarly, the resources in a central processing facility (mainframe) can be counted and tracked because all activity affecting them comes from a single source.

If the definition of the enterprise only included tightly managed corporate resources, the problem of accounting for enterprise assets would not exist. It is the distributed network of diverse desktops and servers that eludes management.

THE SITUATION/PROBLEM

It is not the attributes of the desktops and servers that make them inherently difficult to account for. It is the makeup of our business processes. A client/server architecture evolved from a need for flexibility and a need to react quickly to a rapidly changing business climate. This required empowerment of those closest to the problem. And in most cases, these individuals are not enveloped in any form of centralized enterprise reporting. In the case of managing client/server resources, this translates into a mission-critical resource having multiple sources of change, little accountability, and metamorphic consistency.

All of this is perhaps best illustrated with a diagram that highlights a single desktop and the sources and types of change that may affect its definition as a corporate asset.

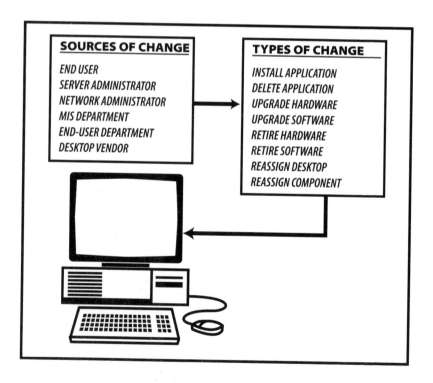

Within this complexity of multiple sources and types of change, the need for basic accountability remains unchanged. How many do I have? What do they look like? And where are they located? Organizations spend millions of dollars ($60–$120 per desktop) every year trying to answer these questions through an annual physical inventory. What's more, these costs often do not include the agonizing effort of attempting to reconcile an inventory across a base of assets that took several months to count, while experiencing significant purchasing and business activity.

THE FIRST STEP

Shortly after implementing an asset tracking solution, assuming you make a proper selection, you will be able to produce an accurate listing of each desktop and server that makes up the enterprise. Collected information includes: the processor type and speed, attached peripherals, add-on cards, software, division, user information, memory complement, and associated server information.

From this baseline of data, you can now generate departmental and division summaries, counts by item type, and a periodic listing of all new items discovered by the asset tracking system. After multiple snapshots have been taken, you can identify equipment and software that are reported as missing and/or retired.

By collecting the newly reported software and equipment data on a cycle that matches interim financial and operating reports, management can track the growth of the enterprise against planned expenditures. By having a current picture of distributed asset activity, management can proactively manage growth in the client/server base around an annual plan, rather than discovering massive overruns at year-end.

Just the Beginning

Once the asset tracking system is implemented, several steps can be taken to make it an integral component of your accounting systems.

By working with your supplier of desktop systems, you can have them "burn" the invoice number into new systems that are shipped to your organization. This reference number would always appear on the desktop at the same location, thus allowing the tracking system to find it and make it part of the snapshot for that system.

Furthermore, any new additions to a desktop (e.g., memory, software, etc.) that do not have an asset identification number and/or invoice number associated with them can be flagged, and the appropriate identifiers can be added to the repository. Tracking assets at this level creates a closed loop between the desktop, asset inventory, and purchasing systems.

Ultimately, the ideal would be to fully integrate the asset tracking system with the fixed-asset accounting system. Although ambitious, this task can be accomplished with relative ease if the selected tracking system maintains a historical base of knowledge and has an open interface to other applications.

Epilogue

An epilogue is included to highlight some of the discoveries that MIS professionals have shared with me in the management of their distributed enterprise.

As a result of implementing an automated asset tracking system, organizations can:

• Reduce the cost of physical inventories from $60 per workstation to zero. In a 10,000-workstation enterprise, this results in a $600,000 savings.

- Proactively track the implementation of distributed IT assets during the year and react to unfavorable purchasing activities (trends) in real time, thereby avoiding year-end budget surprises.

- Give operating management a more precise view of its business operations via departmental/division summaries of distributed IT assets. This allows management to apply the same business metrics to the distributed IT asset base that it applies to other assets.

- Gain a powerful tool in monitoring the activity and integrity of suppliers by linking ("burning" the invoice number into newly ordered systems) them to the asset tracking system. In addition, the tracking of warranty status and installation certification becomes an automatic by-product of the asset tracking solution.

CHAPTER 7
• # NEW DISHES •
SAVINGS/ROI

Judi (my wife): *(Coming home from the store)* You wouldn't believe how much money I saved!

Me: What did you buy?

Wife: New dishes. They were 40 percent off.

Me: Were we in the market for new dishes?

Wife: No, but they were such a great deal I couldn't pass up the savings.

Me: You know honey, you may have a future in Congress.

I tease my wife about this and similar conversations, but in fairness, she really should be in charge of the congressional budget office. I tell this story, not because I have a desire to sleep on the couch tonight, but rather to make a point—an asset tracking system should not be difficult to cost justify. If it is, you never really had a need, or you are looking to justify it the wrong way. Asset tracking is a "Mack truck project." Its benefits are not subtle, and within a distributed enterprise, its cost justification is overwhelmingly persuasive.

To assist in the cost justification process, I have outlined several areas identified by IT executives as areas of substantial savings. I chose these areas because they highlight several different means of quantifying the value of an asset tracking system. Some of the sources of savings are mathematical; some are a "seat-of-your-pants analysis." In some ways the less formal sources are more instructive than their more precise mathematical cousins. These less quantitative savings obtain their informality out of necessity. If the asset tracking information were available, you could, in most cases, precisely calculate the value of acquiring an asset tracking system. Of course, this begs the question of why you would entertain this exercise if you already had an accurate asset tracking system in place.

EXAMPLES OF POTENTIAL SAVINGS/RETURNS

REDUCED COSTS IN CONDUCTING A PHYSICAL INVENTORY

At least once each year a physical inventory is conducted of all corporate assets. This inventory, according to industry consultants, costs between $60 and $120 per desktop, depending on the size of the enterprise, its geographic distribution, and whether the effort is managed in-house or contracted to an outside firm. This would place the cost of inventorying a 10,000-workstation enterprise at between $600,000 and $1,200,000. Keep in mind this is for a single inventory!

At first, these numbers may sound high; however, they fall into line when you consider the direct labor costs associated with conducting a physical inventory. Not included in these numbers are the costs of end-user involvement (lost productivity), travel costs, consolidation and reconciliation of the gathered information, logistics management costs, and the labor associated with managing the gathered data and reporting the results. Considering the labor-intensive nature of many of these tasks, many IT professionals consider a $200 figure to be more representative of the true cost of inventorying a desktop.

VENDOR MANAGEMENT

Many organizations are at the mercy of software vendors when discussing upgrades and new application acquisitions because the vendors' records are the most reliable source of installation information available. One federal government IT executive recently told me he had ordered a 10,000-user upgrade knowing full well that only 3,000 copies were actually installed. His reasoning was simple: the vendor had the most accurate unit count, and the cost of proving them wrong was greater than paying for the incremental 7,000 upgrades.

In the above example, if we assume that the cost per desktop upgrade is $50, and further assume the IT executive is correct in his assessment that only 3,000 of the 10,000 copies would be put into production, then not having an asset tracking system results in an overpayment of $350,000 for the upgrade (7,000 unused upgrades x $50).

There are many variances to this theme and an equal number of ways to compute savings in this area. One way is to construct an average scenario and multiply it by the number of times you would encounter that scenario each year. Better yet, consider how past upgrade or purchasing decisions could have been improved with the availability of asset tracking information and extrapolate your results into future savings.

"HIDDEN COST" MANAGEMENT

Simple actions often have complex cost implications. Most IT executives have been faced with the infamous upgrade "dribble effect." Here a fixed cost is identified for upgrading to the latest revision of a desktop application. After the upgrade is distributed to the user base, the dribble begins. The dribble is comprised of unanticipated CPU upgrades, memory upgrades, disk upgrades, and operating system upgrades. It is not unusual for the aggregate dribble expense to greatly exceed the cost of the software upgrade!

There is no set formula that can be applied across all organizations to determine how much money can be saved through the use of an asset tracking system uncovering hidden costs. However, the potential savings are substantial. Areas of savings include: the upgrades that will be canceled once the fully loaded cost is understood; the money saved through volume purchasing of the necessary upgrade components; end-user time saved from trying to make the new software work on an underconfigured system; and the end-user and staff time saved through the coordination of the desktop upgrades.

Even without a set formula for computing these savings, a conservative estimate can be computed by multiplying the "dribble effect" by a savings factor and using the result as a conservative savings benchmark. For example, if for each dollar spent upgrading application software another dollar is spent on associated dribble expenses (the dribble effect ratio, in this case, is 1:1), and if volume purchasing can reduce costs by 15 percent (savings factor), then you have enough information to compute benchmark savings. The annual "hidden cost" savings from having an asset tracking system would be computed as follows:

```
(AVERAGE UPGRADE COST X DRIBBLE EFFECT RATIO) X
SAVINGS FACTOR X THE NUMBER OF UPGRADES PER YEAR
               = SAVINGS
```

If the average application upgrade is $500,000, the dribble expense ratio is 1:1, the savings factor is 15 percent, and an average of six upgrades occur each year, the benchmark savings would be $450,000 per year ((500,000 x 1) x .15 x 6).

HELP DESK STAFFING COSTS

This one is easy. On average, determine how much time would be saved on the average help desk call if all configuration information was instantly available, showing snapshots of the end-user's machine before and after the problem was experienced. The computation of savings is straightforward:

(TOTAL NUMBER OF CALLS X TIME SAVED PER CALL)
X FULLY LOADED HOURLY RATE FOR HELP DESK
PROFESSIONAL = SAVINGS

Charge-back Capture
(Migration to a Standard Desktop)

As mentioned in chapter 6, an asset tracking system has the ability to provide the information necessary to tie support costs to those resources consuming the support services. As a result, users are naturally encouraged to migrate to supportable configurations. The computation of the benefits of this migration toward standards is subjective. The only formula I ever heard that attempted to quantify this type of savings came from an IT executive who worked for a bank. His formula is based on the belief that a standard desktop costs half as much to support as a non-standard desktop and makes the end users 20 percent more productive. Since he knew the support cost for his end users and the fully loaded end-user rate, he extrapolated the value of moving the desktop 10 percent closer to a desirable standard.

Proactive Management of Known Problems

How often do we read in the press, hear from a software/ hardware vendor, or learn from the help desk group about a problem that will affect end-user productivity? Without an asset tracking system, it is impossible to find those users who will be affected by the known problems. Chapter 5 discusses how the audit function not only can identify users who have a problem configuration, but also can warn users who are likely to upgrade to a problem configuration. The computation of the asset tracking cost benefit in this area is computed by establishing three benchmarks.

Benchmark 1. First, how much downtime do end users experience when they encounter an unexpected problem? This is the average amount of time the end user loses before contacting the help desk; published statistics range from .75 to 1.5 hours.

Benchmark 2. Second, how much time does it take the help desk professional and the end user to identify the source of the problem? This assumes that both the help desk professional and the end user are equally ignorant of the problem source upon first contact; estimates for this benchmark range from .25 to 2.0 hours, depending on the industry and end-user mix.

Benchmark 3. Third, if an auditing function were in place as part of an asset tracking solution, how much help desk time would be required to proactively inform the end user of the problem? Notice that no consideration of the time required to fix the problem is included in this example. It is assumed that once the problem has been identified, regardless of the means of identification, the time required to fix the problem would be constant.

By estimating the number of end-user problems encountered that were previously known via the press, vendors, or help desk, and multiplying the number by the total time lost by end users and help desk staff (see Benchmark 1 and 2 above), we arrive at a total time spent on passively managed problems. Subtract from this the time required for the help desk and end user to proactively manage the same situation (see Benchmark 3 above), and you arrive at the incremental time required to passively manage the known problem set. Multiply this incremental time by the fully loaded hourly rates for both the end user and help desk professional, and you have computed the savings of proactively managing known problems.

REDISTRIBUTION OF IDLE ASSETS

One of the least considered, yet potentially powerful, uses of an asset tracking system is the discovery and redistribution of idle IT assets. Desktop systems and servers are often unofficially "taken out of service" for a variety of reasons, including: the restructuring of the business unit, employee transition, technology shifts, technology upgrades, and equipment failure. Most organizations have some form of surplus equipment depot; however, because of the dynamic nature of the business enterprise and geographic obstacles, it is difficult to maintain any form of count, location, or configuration of equipment not in service. Often, equipment is stored until obsolete or it is "cannibalized" and absorbed into the user base.

An active asset tracking system has the ability to detect when equipment does not report during its most recent snapshot window, allowing for immediate investigation as to the status of the asset. In addition, through the use of configuration flags, such as a byte count of available online storage, the tracking system can detect systems that are not currently active. This set of asset tracking features allows for the creation of a "virtual" surplus equipment depot of all unused or inactive assets. These assets can be redeployed as complete systems, tracked and redeployed as individual hardware and software components, or returned to a centralized depot for repair and/or redeployment.

The value of surplus equipment and the savings derived from maintaining an accurate accounting of inactive resources is largely organization specific. Typically, organizations that receive the greatest benefit from an asset tracking system in this area are those that have a span of user requirements for varying levels of technology. Within such organizations, finding utility for idle assets is simply a matter of identifying the business function that uses that level of technology (easy to find using an asset tracking system) and notifying that unit of its availability. Distribution of component parts is dependent on the base of technology and the plug-and-play nature of the components.

Measuring the precise cost savings from the tracking of these resources is accomplished by estimating the percentage of new software and hardware procurements that might be met via an asset recapture program. I have heard of estimates as low as .5 percent and as high as 20 percent. Depending on the nature of your business, and the value of new IT acquisitions each year, the savings can easily range from hundreds of thousands to millions of dollars.

IMPROVEMENTS IN BUSINESS OPERATIONS

As each business is unique, it is impossible to produce a formula that calculates the value of an asset tracking system as it relates to specific business operations. Needless to say, however, the greatest cost justification of an asset tracking system is found in this area. Asset tracking has the potential to allow a tighter integration of suppliers and customers into the enterprise. This can translate into improved margins, expanded market share, and more efficient business operations. A brief example of how asset tracking can be integrated into business operations is provided in Case Study 2.

STORED, LOST, OR STOLEN ASSETS

Like it or not, technology has become currency. Processors, memory chips, disk drives, CD-ROM drives, video cards, and printers have known and published cash equivalents.

A good friend of mine, who is a recognized leader in enterprise technology, recently illustrated the vulnerability of our IT asset base when he asked me the following questions: "Ounce for ounce, what is worth more, gold or that new notebook computer? Ounce for ounce, what is worth more, gold or that stack of memory chips? Would you leave a $5,000 chunk of gold sitting out on an open desk? If you did leave it there, would you check on it periodically?" Having never thought of IT assets in those terms, his questions awakened my interest in the mobility and liquidity of distributed IT assets.

As I began to make inquiries of IT professionals and other business managers, I discovered that many of them had already recognized the threat and had experienced losses. These losses came from a variety of sources, including: employees upgrading their home systems by swapping components with their work desktop; theft of components by contract employees; theft of complete desktops by cleaning service employees; and ordered, invoiced, and paid-for equipment that never found its way to the enterprise.

As discussed in chapter 3, an asset tracking system has the ability to make all parties aware that the assets are being watched, and allow you to react quickly to losses before they proliferate. The question is: How do you quantify this benefit as part of the justification of an asset tracking system? Corporate security or an outside security consultant is a good place to start, as they often have published statistics on the theft rate of various assets across industry segments. With such information available (e.g., your industry estimates a .5 percent loss of the high-tech asset base over a twelve-month period), your security expert can assist you in calculating the value of actively tracking the distributed asset base and, from this, a range of potential savings can be extrapolated.

I strongly encourage you to consider the potential savings/return from improved security for the distributed IT asset base. Consider the following: If you have 10,000 distributed desktops and servers with an average depreciated replacement value of $3,500 each and an assumed 1 percent loss rate over a twelve-month period, your losses will be $350,000.

The loss of the physical asset, however, is only the beginning. What is the associated productivity loss of the end users who lose their desktops? What is the administrative cost of purchasing the replacement, investigating the loss, and recovering the information that disappeared with the asset? These expenses can far exceed the replacement cost of the physical asset.

EMPOWERMENT OF OTHER IT ASSETS

To compute the savings/return through the empowerment of other IT assets, it is best to examine the original justification for the empowered asset and determine how the addition of an asset tracking system enhances that justification. For example, assume that part of the justification for the new help desk system installed last year was improved end-user productivity through rapid problem resolution. By using these projected savings as a base, you can calculate the incremental value of implementing an asset tracking system. More simply stated, if the benefit of quick problem resolution was calculated to improve end-user productivity by $5 million, and an asset tracking system improves response by an additional 20 percent, then the empowerment provided by asset tracking would logically be valued at $1 million.

SUMMARY

Valuing knowledge is an art, valuing utility is a science, but insight defies valuation, for its wisdom enriches all that rests within its grasp.

CHAPTER 8
• ALUMINUM SIDING •
HIDDEN COSTS

Me: So what kind of money are we talking about?

Aluminum Siding Salesman: How does $486 sound?

Me: For both the front and back gables?

Aluminum Siding Salesman: Yes.

Me: Sounds great. When can you begin?

Aluminum Siding Salesman: If you sign a contract today, I can have a crew out here Monday. Just sign here…

Me: Do I get to read it first?

Aluminum Siding Salesman: It's just a standard sales agreement.

Me: What does "plus installation and transport fees" mean?

Aluminum Siding Salesman: It means there is a small additional fee for those items.

Me: And what are those fees?

Aluminum Siding Salesman: There is a standard $500 installation fee for a job this size and a nominal $90 shipping fee.

Me: I think you had better nominal yourself off my property.

The contractor I eventually selected to install the siding charged me a flat $500; his contract was my promise to pay him if he did a good job. The simplicity of this transaction died twenty years ago. Today, we are faced with a bewildering cascade of options as we consider even the most basic of buying decisions. Suppliers of goods and services, in their zeal to attract profitable business, design and package items in an ever-more-confusing manner.

Today, even simple items like car advertisements contain qualifiers that are worthy of a Mideast peace negotiation. "Drive this beauty home for $219 per month!" the ad screams in 120-point type. Down below in nine-point type, we read "(required advance payment of $1,380, 48-month closed-end lease, assumes 8,000 miles per year, customer responsible for lease origination, title, taxes, dealer prep, transfer, and delivery fees)." I have a real ambivalence about the fine print in these ads—I'm happy they are providing disclosure, but sad that disclosure is necessary.

This chapter is my capitulation to the current system; it is the small print that should appear at the bottom of every asset tracking proposal. It discloses the potential hidden and other costs associated with implementing an asset tracking system. Unfortunately, my depth of expertise and the targeted size of this book force me to document only a partial list of disclosures. I encourage you to look beyond these considerations when calculating the true cost of ownership, as the unique nature of your business or enterprise may generate issues that have an equally profound impact on the total cost of implementing an asset tracking system.

Before moving to a panorama of considerations (disclosures), it is useful to define the universe of asset tracking systems. Asset tracking systems are generally priced on a per-seat (desktop/server) basis, with licenses ranging from $15 per seat to $250 per seat. A logical assumption would be that the more expensive products offer a richer set of product features or an overall lower cost of ownership; however, some of the lower-priced solutions lay claim to these distinctions.

So what do you get for the higher price? In some cases you get "customization" that is unique to your business. In some cases you get "customization" that provides features already available in lower-priced products as a standard. And in some cases you receive extensive installation support and/or leasing services. All of this can be confusing, and if it were not, this chapter would be unnecessary. The remainder of this chapter provides a list of considerations, which, if addressed, will force vendors to reveal many of the hidden and associated costs that are inherent in the purchase and implementation of their products.

CONSIDERATIONS

HIDDEN SOFTWARE UPGRADES

The biggest hidden cost of implementing an asset tracking system is the cost of upgrading the enterprise to support the application. Some operating system vendors and network management vendors offer attractive pricing on the asset tracking component; however, when all the prerequisites are considered, the pricing is no longer so attractive.

To avoid this surprise, a list of the recommended (not minimal) "supporting" or prerequisite software should be supplied in writing by each vendor early in the decision process. In some cases, the cost of "application enabling" (upgrading) the network is five times the cost of the asset tracking application. Before dismissing the potential impact of this hidden cost, ask yourself the following question: What would it cost to upgrade the operating system on all of my servers? Don't forget the cost of the upgrade, testing, installation support, and training.

HIDDEN HARDWARE UPGRADES

Closely tied to the cost of hidden software upgrades is the associated cost of hardware required to implement those upgrades.

Even smart buyers who uncover and include the cost of the software prerequisites often fail to consider the implications that software has on the hardware resources. Typically, this is not caught during benchmarking or testing of the asset tracking system because the testing is run in a lab environment on a dedicated machine. The performance flaw in hardware configuration is not discovered until the upgraded software and asset tracking application are put into production and an incremental load is placed on the distributed servers and workstations. The solution is to load all of the required software on two production servers and their associated workstations, and then test the viability of the existing hardware and proposed software. Obviously, any hardware upgrades become part of the cost base when considering various asset tracking solutions.

TOOLS VERSUS SOLUTIONS

Some of the most expensive asset tracking systems are tools, not solutions. They deliver a framework of functionality that is tailored to the requirements of the customer. On the surface, these solutions appear to have an attractive purchase price, but in reality, the application is a Trojan horse for the vendor's consulting group. In many cases, the delivered "customized capabilities" are standard features in competitive products, and thus you end up paying premium rates for standard features. In addition, as this type of implementation is typically built on a proprietary architecture, it has the added disadvantage of tying you to a specific consulting resource. Should you decide to implement an asset tracking solution around this paradigm, at a minimum, you should make certain that the tool set is sufficiently documented and accessible to allow for competitive bids for any future customization of the product.

TRAINING PROGRAMS

Here is a case where comprehensive is not desirable. An extensive training program that is included as part of an asset tracking proposal should raise a red flag. Remember: ideally, an asset tracking system should be transparent to the end user and server administrator, intuitive and easily "tuned" by those responsible for the system, and should require little or no administration. Any training provided should be primarily directed toward those installing and modifying the system. Extensive training requirements outside these two exceptions are cause for investigation.

ASSET TRACKING SYSTEM PRICING

There are three basic components of asset tracking pricing: the cost of the software, the cost of maintenance, and the cost of updates/upgrades. Each should be considered when computing the cost of a system.

Typically, the software costs are structured around workstation pricing. Within this structure, there are variances, including: renewable twelve-month licenses, metered usage, perpetual licenses, and fees that are tied to other services such as leasing. Beware of asset tracking solutions that are tied to other services as they may hide substantial costs within other services. For example, a leasing service may provide some limited asset inventory information as part of a leasing service. This may be cost-effective as long as the leasing rates are attractive; however, should you be forced to accept higher lease rates in return for having access to asset information, you may end up paying a premium rate for an inferior asset tracking solution.

Since asset tracking is at the heart of enterprise management, the structure and price of a maintenance program must be considered. Types of maintenance programs include: per-minute support fees, annual maintenance fees based on the size of the installed base of desktops, and dedicated on-site support. Care should be taken to equalize support offerings as levels of service vary from vendor to vendor. Typically, levels of service revolve around some combination of patches (bug fixes), maintenance releases, and enhancement releases (new revisions).

Of special consideration when evaluating pricing of a maintenance program is the cost of new releases, because the pace within the IT enterprise mirrors the product life cycles of the components it tracks. As new hardware, software, and peripherals are introduced to the market and are added to the enterprise, the selected system must be enhanced to recognize and report on those new components. Given the frequency of change, it is highly desirable to have these enhancements included within the maintenance fee. In some cases, such as those systems that are based on a consulting paradigm, this will not be possible as each change requires a consulting effort. If new releases are not bundled into a flat-fee maintenance program, care should be taken to include the cost of multiple annual updates as part of the price evaluation.

Deployment and Update Costs

As a general rule, you can expect the cost of deployment to exceed the cost of the application. The initial installation of the product may be as simple as having the end user insert a diskette into the desktop, or as complex as sending out an IT professional to install and reconfigure each desktop and server. The effort required, and the associated costs of this initial installation, can be easily ascertained during product evaluations and should be included in any product price comparisons.

More important than the cost of initial installation is the cost of applying updates to the desktops. As new revisions of the asset tracking software are released, allowing for the tracking of new software and technology, the cost of performing updates becomes significant. There is a substantial variance in the cost and effort required to perform updates. Some systems automatically update the desktops and servers as part of taking a snapshot of the enterprise, while other systems require an IT professional to install and reconfigure the update on each desktop and server. Considering that each desktop may need to be updated several times each year, the effort and expense associated with each update should receive special consideration.

COST OF INTEGRATING RESULTS

Some asset tracking systems do not automatically create a central repository of the enterprise assets. Systems with this architecture (e.g., LAN-based asset tracking solutions) require some form of consolidation and reconciliation of the asset information that is collected from the various collection points. Depending on the tool set provided for this consolidation, the size of the enterprise, and the frequency of collection, substantial resources may be required to track and merge collection points into a central repository. Costs involved in this calculation include the time expended by the IT professionals managing the central collection effort and the time expended by those reading the data at the various collection points.

If you are considering a LAN-based asset tracking solution to manage your enterprise, special care must be taken in the administration of the solution. The consolidation of the information from the various collection points must be coordinated and verified to avoid duplication of asset information or corruption of the repository. If this is your selected methodology, it would be wise to dedicate experienced staff to the reconciliation effort.

COST OF CUSTOM REPORTING

As mentioned in chapter 6, the real value of an effective asset tracking system lies in the accessibility of the information. Accordingly, the cost of extracting that information should be considered. If each individual using the system must rely on a consultant or IT professional each time an information need falls outside the provided standard reports, the cost of providing these resources must be quantified. There is a full range of possibilities in this area—from systems that provide novice users with almost unlimited reporting capabilities to systems that have closed data structures and do not allow for non-standard reporting.

COST OF DATA ACCESSIBILITY
(EASY TO UNDERSTAND AND ACCESS)

Ideally, the asset repository would be a relational database that is open database compliant (ODBC), allowing unlimited flexibility in the formatting and extraction of information. At the other end of the spectrum is a closed, fixed-format architecture that is accessible only by the vendor supplying the application. This issue may seem like a technical detail, but it is quintessential to establishing the cost of utility. Flexible access to the asset tracking repository is critical to empowering other applications, developing ad hoc inquiries, modeling, and auditing the enterprise. The greatest cost of not having easy access to the asset tracking repository is the inability to extract the information required to make an informed decision.

The frustration of "information starvation" takes two primary forms: first, the information is not available, and second, the time and resources required to extract the information obviates its utility.

To determine the accessibility of an asset tracking repository, ask the vendor giving the demonstration to show you how to produce (extract) several different types of information that are not part of a standard query or reporting facility. If this requires extensive vendor support, you should build substantial consulting fees into the cost model. If the information cannot be produced, you should consider another asset tracking system.

The Cost of Change

The "required information" extracted from and associated with the desktops and servers is a moving target. As new technology is implemented, business practices change, organizations evolve, and new enterprise management tools are deployed. As a result, the definition of what must be discovered, tracked, and associated with the desktops and servers undergoes a metamorphosis. The cost of making these changes should be considered when selecting an asset tracking system.

The greatest cost in this area is not that of making the change, but rather the inability to make the necessary additions and modifications to keep the repository in harmony with the organization. This inability can result in the asset tracking system becoming unable to conform to the structure of your business (e.g., a new division code cannot be associated with the desktops), unable to collect the information that enables other applications, or unable to report on a critical new piece of technology that is being added to the enterprise.

Determining the cost of modifying the system requires that you address three different types of change. First, investigate the internal and external resources required to add a new Phantom Comparative Anchor (see chapter 3) to the information associated with the desktop or server. Second, investigate the internal and external resources required to recognize a new physical asset (e.g., a new communications card) that is being deployed throughout the enterprise. And third, investigate the internal and external resources required to recognize and report on a new software package that is being deployed across the enterprise. Questions that need to be addressed for each of the three types of change include the following: Are such modifications possible? Are they practical? Can your MIS staff make these changes? Is there a documented standard that allows you to competitively outsource the changes? And, what is required to integrate these changes into the asset repository?

Don't forget that once you make these changes, you need to deploy them across the enterprise. Make certain each type of change discussed above is included in your analysis of "Deployment and Update Costs" covered earlier in this chapter.

COST OF ADMINISTRATION

Depending on the answers to the questions raised in this chapter and technology considerations (see chapter 13), the cost of administering the system may or may not be a significant factor. Primary areas of concern in determining administration cost include: the amount of end-user involvement, the amount of server administrator involvement, the effort required to change the system, frequency of changes to the system, the outside resources required to maintain the system, and the ease of extracting and transferring meaningful information to other applications and to decision makers.

The quantification of administration costs should be one of the final steps in your evaluation. After you complete your other analyses, make a list of the features, functions, justifications, and architectural components of the considered asset tracking system. Beside each line item, indicate the required administrative effort. With this list you can build an administration cost estimate.

SUMMARY

The true cost of an item is not discovered in its price, but in its use.

CHAPTER 9

• **MTV STUDY GUIDE** •

THE INTERNET

Me: What are you doing?

Rachel (my daughter): Homework.

Me: Why is the TV on?

Rachel: It helps me study.

Me: What are you watching?

Rachel: MTV.

Me: How does that help you study?

Rachel: It's complicated. You wouldn't understand.

Me: What are you working on?

Rachel: Algebra...I'll turn it off.

It seems silly that my daughter Rachel would view MTV as some form of a study aid, as the MTV format is by design a fast-paced, free-form, quick-cutting montage of movement and color designed to capture and hold your attention. Who but a fifteen-year-old could possibly consider this a productivity tool?

As we muse at Rachel's lack of perspective, we should be cautious in our derision, for we decision makers of Corporate America are putting an MTV competitor on the desktops in our enterprises. It too goes by three initials—WWW (World Wide Web). To eliminate confusion between the terms "Internet" and "Intranet," I will refer to the Internet as the WWW throughout the remainder of this text.

I know how unpopular it is to question the boundless productivity offered by the WWW, yet dozens of senior executives have confided in me that one of their greatest productivity problems is the misuse of this very resource.

To be certain, the WWW is a tool with vast potential; however, this potential is sharpened on both edges. As obviously as the positive aspects of the WWW present themselves, the flaws are equally good at hiding. To understand the impact that uncontrolled end-user access to the WWW can have on an organization, consider the following:

An average user, with a fully loaded cost of $105 per hour who spends twenty minutes per day surfing the WWW on non-job-related topics, will cost his employer $8,750 per year in unproductive expense. Multiply this by 10,000 Web-empowered employees, and even this moderate case of "Web waste" results in an unproductive salary expense of more than $87 million! This doesn't even account for the cost of lost productivity (lost opportunity cost), which could easily triple the impact.

Because of the "richness" of WWW resources, employees are increasingly overresearching even the simplest information needs. I recently asked one of my senior managers to find out the annual revenues of a prospective business partner. My need to know this information was driven by my desire to mentally slot them into one of our existing programs. By knowing their current revenues, I could easily determine the level of resources they would consume and the type of training they would require.

Several hours later, the senior manager returned with a stack of paper three inches thick on the company in question. Included in this stack of information were sections that had been marked with a highlighter and numerous notes in the margin. This manager, empowered by the MTV-like flash of the WWW, had explored the WWW for my answer and found the jewel I desired, as well as a vast treasure of information not requested. The price of this excursion was more than $500 in unproductive expense.

The WWW also has the power to diminish the productivity of those individuals who use discipline in their WWW activity or who do not use the WWW at all. In the above example, the senior manager overresearched a simple data request, wasting $500 of salary and productivity expense. The impact of this waste did not end there, however, for he sent copies of his research to three other managers including me. Much to my regret, I skimmed the entire packet of information, actually reading the highlighted areas and margin notes. I later discovered the other managers did the same. In the final analysis, I did get the revenue number I requested, but at a dear price. Collectively, the two other senior managers and I spent one and a half hours reading information that was not requested and that was of limited value. Each of us would have been far more productive spending that time on our core jobs.

The total price tag for this single effort of overresearch was more than $800. If this seems like an anomaly to you, I would encourage you to look at the number of attachments to your e-mail traffic. E-mail is the perfect carrier for this infectious waste of productivity, and most of us find it difficult not to pop open those attachments when sent from someone we respect.

One of the most fascinating aspects of the WWW is that its availability is predicated on self-interest, rather than profit. That is to say, providers of information on the WWW do not do so in order to promote the WWW or receive a royalty; instead, they have a single selfish interest—to make their "story" (information) available to others.

This availability of free information often positions the WWW as a source of news and reference material. In many cases this label is accurate, but increasingly, organizations are discovering that much of the research extracted from the WWW is biased and/or highly suspect. If we detach ourselves from the Web hysteria for a moment, the reason for all of the suspect information is obvious. There is no profit motive to keep things honest.

Every credible news source has an underlying need for accuracy. If they report false information on a regular basis, the public will stop buying their product and they will cease to exist. Not so on the WWW where anyone who has a point of view can publish an opinion that may be masked as a research document encased in credentials nearly impossible to verify.

As a result, organizations are increasingly monitoring the information sources used by their employees. This monitoring is targeted toward two objectives. First, to ensure the organization has an accurate base of facts on which to make a decision. And second, to prevent their most valuable assets, their employees, from wasting time with resources that will later be discounted—or worse yet—lead to wrong decisions.

End-user productivity is increasingly tied to the network of clients and servers known as the Intranet. The Intranet is the internal web of communications lines, bridges, routers, and modems that allow these clients and servers to communicate at high speeds (e.g., 1.5 million bits per second).

Joining the internal Intranet to the outside world of the WWW is a gateway. This gateway allows internal users, attached to the Intranet, to access the "free" outside resources of the WWW. The diagram on the following page begins to illuminate how this "free resource" can cost an organization millions or even tens of millions of dollars each year.

This diagram highlights the vast resources separating the users from the WWW. This conglomeration of resources, the Intranet, is responsible for carrying the traffic of the organization's mission-critical applications. Organizations spend vast sums of money to ensure that there is bandwidth to carry this mission-critical traffic and to provide a rapid response to its end users.

The same resources that carry the mission-critical traffic also carry extraneous Internet traffic. Thus, many organizations that are not in control of Internet usage find themselves with unexplained degradation of their Intranet, and are forced to upgrade Intranet resources in an effort to maintain adequate response times and throughput for mission-critical applications.

Consider the impact that a single use of the WWW might have on a 300-user finance department. Assume for a moment the popular PointCast Network screen saver application, which allows the latest news and stock quotes to colorfully scroll across your screen when the desktop is in a screen saver mode, became a desktop favorite. Of the 300 users in finance, 220 elected to access the PointCast Network application once each hour (the default setting). Since the typical download of a PointCast Network update is in excess of 150,000 bytes, this single use of the WWW will put a 33-million-byte burden per hour on the Intranet resources serving the finance department. In addition, it will put a similar burden on all the communications resources between the communications server that links finance to the Intranet and the gateway that provides access to the WWW.

Although this 33-million-byte hourly load may not seem significant, it only represents a single use of WWW resources. In addition, considering the number of business transactions that can be transferred in 33 million bytes, and the impact that the PointCast Network application may have on response times, it becomes clear that WWW traffic can lead to costly upgrades of Intranet resources.

TAMING THE NET

This discussion may lead you to believe that I am against plugging users into the WWW. Although it is true that some users would be well served by having their access to the WWW blocked, I am a strong proponent of making the WWW available to the majority of users. This assumes there are reasonable controls in place, allowing policies to be monitored and enforced. In reality, the WWW is a resource not unlike a long-distance phone service. Not all callers need access to the WWW, just as not all callers need access to international long-distance service.

If reasonable control of the WWW is to be exercised, you must be able to:

1) Associate WWW traffic with individual users.

2) Understand trends in WWW usage.

3) Determine what WWW resources are being used.

If this information is known, the WWW can be used with few or none of the problems discussed earlier. It should not be surprising that an effective asset tracking system can be invaluable in gathering and presenting actionable WWW usage analyses.

WEB FINGERPRINTS

As mentioned earlier, access to the WWW is attained through the Intranet via a gateway. This gateway, in addition to providing access to the WWW, records the activity that passes through it. This activity log would be nothing but a numeric jumble of transactions of fingerprints if it were not for the asset repository. The asset repository can apply these transactions to individual users, departments, or divisions and collect and sort them by type of activity.

An asset tracking system has the ability to capture and apply the raw data fingerprints left behind by WWW activity. This raw fingerprint data includes: the time of day the WWW request was made, the network address making the request, the site accessed (e.g., Disney, General Motors, SEC), all pages (specific pieces of information from the site), and the number of bytes transferred as a result of each query. In processing this amalgamation of information, the asset tracking system sorts and associates each transaction with the existing base of knowledge on workstations, servers, and end users. Once processed, the asset tracking system presents its results from several different perspectives, enabling proactive control of both user productivity and network productivity as they relate to WWW activity.

UNDERSTANDING WWW ACTIVITY

To understand the meaning of WWW activity, you must focus on five factors. Each of these factors, separately and in combination, is required to effectively manage WWW activity. These factors include:

1) *What sites are being accessed?* This information includes not only the top sites accessed by the organization, department/division, and individual, but also the number of different sites being accessed. Here is the best macro-measurement of how the WWW is being used: Is the number one site for your finance department Dow Jones or Disney?

2) *What pages are being requested?* Here the specific information that your users are consuming is discovered. The most frequently accessed site by your marketing department may be the *Wall Street Journal*, but if 80 percent of the accesses to this site are for the sports scores page, you may not be getting the desired utility out of your WWW resources.

3) *What time is the WWW activity taking place?* It has been said that timing is everything, and WWW usage confirms this axiom. Knowing that your sales department has a substantial number of accesses to an interactive golf simulation page may not be disturbing if accessed during lunch hours, but may be unacceptable at 3:00 P.M. The timing of WWW activity is especially critical when network issues are being addressed.

4) *What is the trend of WWW activity?* Almost all WWW activity is best viewed across time. Is usage over time on the increase, or is this month's activity an anomaly?

5) *How much information is being transferred?* A user in the shipping department may only access the Disney site four times per month; however, each access may result in the downloading of 20-million-byte animation files during peak traffic hours.

These five factors provide the keys to understanding the utility of the WWW within your organization. The power of combining these factors with other information in the asset tracking repository is best illustrated in Case Study 5.

SUMMARY

It is a half-educated man who sees opportunity in adversity while ignoring the mishap of good fortune.

CASE STUDY 5
SNARED IN THE NET

Prologue

RMS Capital is a worldwide firm providing financial services to major corporations. Its services include leasing, facilities management, and financial advisory services. Because RMS Capital's business is based solely on employee productivity, a senior manager roundtable is held each quarter to explore ways to improve employee productivity. The meeting is held in turn, with each senior manager having the opportunity to host and control the topics of discussion. This meeting is chaired by Susan Chin, chief information officer for RMS Capital.

Enterprise Definition

RMS Capital has an enterprise of approximately 18,000 desktops that are connected via 3,400 servers. The network consists of a home-office site that represents 14,000 of the desktops with the balance of the units distributed across twenty-three regional worldwide facilities.

Because RMS Capital's business relies on information-based financial services, it values the power of automation and devotes a substantial portion of expenditures to maintaining and upgrading IT resources. Two such upgrades—implementation of an asset tracking system and providing users with access to the WWW—were implemented within the past year.

The Situation/Problem

Although RMS Capital is growing, its rate of growth and sales productivity have declined in the two most recent quarters. Reasons attributed to this decline include: increased competitive pressures, weak product positioning, a change in the sales force compensation package, and the economy.

Other departments within the company have experienced similar sags in their productivity numbers. It is for these reasons that Susan Chin has decided to focus this quarter's roundtable on encouraging departments to use the WWW as a means of boosting productivity.

THE FIRST STEP

Susan begins by running a series of analyses on WWW activity for the most recent months. She suspects that employees may be timid about using the Internet, which is causing them to fall behind their competitors. The information highlighted in the analyses is not what Susan expected. In fact in some cases the WWW seems to be overused, resulting in decreased productivity. Susan decides to focus the entire roundtable session on productivity issues surrounding the WWW.

TRACKING DOWN THE PROBLEM

Susan calls the meeting to order, announcing the agenda and distributing copies of the first analysis. *Note: Although such an analysis would ideally appear on a single page, this chapter presents the sections in a series.*

INTERNET ACCESS ANALYSIS – SUMMARY

The first section of the Internet Access Analysis displays summary information on page and site activity. With more than 7.8 million page accesses for the current month, all managers gain an understanding of how pervasive WWW use has become within RMS Capital.

SUMMARY

There are 13,449 workstations that report Internet activity during the specified period. These workstations connected to 10,659 sites and accessed 7,825,693 pages, including 2,738,993 unique pages.

INTERNET ACCESS ANALYSIS – USAGE BREAKDOWN

Once this information is known, the next logical question is, who is using it? The analysis anticipates this question, providing an insightful usage table.

INTERNET USAGE						
DEPARTMENT	FINANCE	IT	MKTG	SERVICE	SALES	ADMIN
TOTAL WORKSTATIONS (#)	3887	1866	2644	933	3420	2799
TOTAL WORKSTATIONS (%)	25%	12%	17%	6%	22%	18%
WORKSTATIONS ON THE INTERNET(%)	100%	90%	100%	15%	100%	60%
PAGE ACCESSES (#)	2034680	1408625	939083	0	2973763	469542
AVG ACCESS PER WORKSTATION (#)	523	839	355	0	869	280
PAGE ACCESSES (% OF TOTAL)	26%	18%	12%	0%	38%	6%
UNIQUE PAGES (#)	712138	493019	328679	0	1040817	164340
UNIQUE SITES (#)	2503	1733	1155	0	3658	578
TOP TEN USERS (%)	50%	80%	40%	0%	90%	30%

It is from this table that Ben Houser, vice president of sales, discovers the first anomaly concerning WWW usage. Ben points out that although his group makes up only 22 percent of the workstation population (line 2), they make up 38 percent of all WWW page accesses (line 6). Clearly, sales has a high activity level on the WWW. Other managers identify additional areas of interest, but Ben, citing the recent drop in sales productivity, directs them back to his group's issue. He notes that ten of his users are especially active in that they make up 90 percent of all pages accessed by sales (line 9).

Since sales productivity has been such a priority at RMS, everyone agrees to explore the sales department's use of the WWW before considering other WWW issues.

INTERNET ACCESS ANALYSIS – HOURLY PAGE ACCESS

Ben's next question deals with timing, as his group often works on proposals in early morning and late evening hours. Addressing this question in the following section, the analysis displays the month's page activity by department across a twenty-four-hour period.

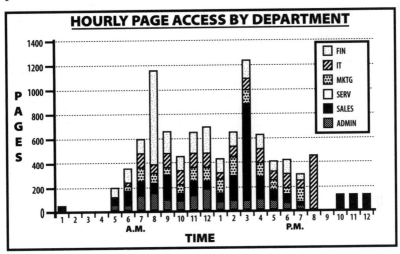

Reviewing this chart, Ben discovers no heavily weighted sales department use at the beginning or end of the days, but rather a fairly uniform distribution. He also discovers an extraordinary spike in page accesses at 3:00 P.M. This is especially unusual because this is the time of day he expects his staff to be in front of the customer. Ben decides to investigate the reason for the spike at 3:00 P.M. and the unusual activity between 10:00 P.M. and midnight.

INTERNET ACCESS ANALYSIS – DEPARTMENTAL PAGE ACCESS

Realizing these results may be a function of some special project or circumstance, Ben consults the next section of the analysis that highlights a six-month trend in usage for each department.

In reviewing the usage curves, Ben observes that, not only does he have a potential problem, but the problem is growing with each passing month. Susan concludes that most groups' use of the WWW has stabilized or declined as the novelty diminished. Ted

Dunmore, CFO, notes that the increased use in the finance department may be due to two new services recently made available to the financial analysts. Ben indicates that to the best of his knowledge, no new services have been acquired for the sales department and asks for a report detailing the specific page activity by department.

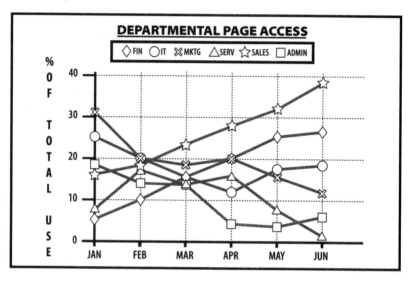

In the course of the meeting, Susan provides Ben with an analysis revealing that the majority of sales department usage is being consumed playing an interactive Space Wars game. Further investigation reveals that the Space Wars tournament started promptly at 3:00 P.M. each afternoon. Susan also produces an analysis, showing the top twenty-five consumers of pages within the company, also known as "Page Hogs." To no one's surprise, thirteen of the twenty-five "Page Hogs" were in sales.

Susan also provides all managers with additional insight into their departments' WWW usage by producing a "Site Hog" analysis and a "Network Hog" analysis. This last analysis is instrumental in clearing up a network bottleneck. The analysis reveals that the bottleneck was caused by users who were regularly downloading sexually explicit graphics during the batch distribution of operating reports across the Intranet.

Finally, Susan distributes to the appropriate managers a personal profile of usage for each employee who appears on one of the "hog" analyses. These detailed profiles reveal that more than half of the "hogs" were primarily using the WWW for personal interests.

EPILOGUE

An epilogue is included in this hypothetical case study to highlight some of the discoveries that MIS professionals have shared with me in the management of their distributed enterprise.

The above roundtable review of the WWW analyses results in the following actions and decisions:

• A formal policy is published and made part of the employee handbook. End users are informed that WWW activity is actively monitored and that appropriate action will be taken against employees violating the established guidelines for WWW usage.

• The Internet gateway is configured to block a list of sites that contain offensive or non-productive material.

• The network management group is assigned the task of reviewing the WWW network traffic analyses each month. They are charged with submitting a monthly report, recommending network-intensive sites that should be blocked and hours during which Internet access should be restricted. As a result of the recommendations, in the first sixty days of this program, two substantial network upgrades were avoided.

• Internet access is blocked from 37 percent of the desktops that failed to justify their need for Web services. The sales department reduces the number of connected users by 45 percent.

• The benefits of the WWW are reintroduced to the customer services group in an effort to give them greater access to customer information and improve customer response times. It is discovered that their decline in WWW use is tied to a network-loading conflict, which was easily resolved by rescheduling downloads during off hours.

• Sales productivity began to show substantial improvement within weeks of implementing the above policies.

From Theory to Application

In theory, all of the above outcomes were made possible by the analyses reporting on WWW activity. In reality, the success attained in managing the WWW had more to do with the basic functions of asset tracking than sorting and summarizing raw gateway data. Clearly, it was assigning this processed data to business entities (Phantom Comparative Anchors) that illuminated its meaning. It was comparing the values of the raw gateway data to other tracked information (Reflective Comparative Anchors) that provided a relative understanding of the problem. It was maintaining and associating this information over a period of time (Trends Comparative Anchor) that allowed managers to focus on escalating problems rather than apparitions. Finally, it was associating this same raw data with those consuming the WWW resources (Phantom Comparative Anchor) that allowed corrective action to be taken.

CHAPTER 10

• BLANKETED ELEPHANTS •

THE YEAR 2000 PROBLEM DEFINED[1]

Me: *(10:30 P.M. at the Springfield airport after a flight from Chicago)* Could you take me to the Ramada Inn next to the hospital, please?

Taxi Driver: In Springfield?

Me: Yes.

Taxi Driver: Sorry buddy, but I've been hacking in Springfield twenty-five years and there ain't no such place.

Me: I have it right here on my itinerary, 147 Trail Street.

Taxi Driver: Sorry, don't know Trail Street either.

Me: *(Irritated)* Wait here. I have a phone number. I'll call for directions.

Phone Operator: I'm sorry sir, but that is not a valid exchange. What area code are you calling?

Me: Two one seven.

Phone Operator: Sir, that is an Illinois area code. Do you want me to connect you to a long-distance operator?

Me: What state is this?

Operator: Missouri.

Me: Never mind.

[1] From Chris Jesse's *Teaching Chipmunks to Dance: The Business Leaders' Guide to Making the Distributed Enterprise Year 2000 Compliant*, Kendall/Hunt Publishing Company (Dubuque, 1997).

Anyone who has traveled extensively has experienced a "near miss" in getting on the wrong plane. Unfortunately, I skipped the "near" part and actually boarded a plane that took me to Springfield, Missouri, instead of Springfield, Illinois. After several hours of driving (to Springfield, Illinois), my boss and I ended up having to share the last available room at the Pioneer Motor Lodge.

This would seem to be a good place to end this story, except for the suspect nature of our quarters that night. Our room was hard to describe; it was actually more of a conference room than a bedroom. As you entered, the first things you noticed were eighty folding chairs arranged in ten rows. Behind the chairs were two folding screens, and behind those, a pair of twin beds and the door to the bathroom. This, of course, seemed odd to us, but most things seem odd at 2:30 in the morning. So we set the alarm for 7:30 A.M. and went to sleep.

As it turned out, we would not need the alarm, for at 6:30 A.M. we found ourselves standing next to our beds at attention, in our underwear, hearts pounding, as we listened to a man with the advantage of a very capable audio system announce the opening and closing prices for hog bellies. I (still in my underwear) peered around the edge of the screen and discovered several things: first, there were eighty farmers gathered in our hotel room for their weekly Pork Producers Meeting; second, exiting the room required me to walk down the center aisle and turn left directly in front of the podium in order to reach the door; and third, certain elephants can indeed hide under blankets.

The hidden elephant I faced back in 1975 was that I had landed in the wrong state and was sleeping in what was obviously a conference room. The hidden elephant we address today is managing the Year 2000 across the distributed enterprise. Ironically, these two different elephants both successfully hid under a common blanket—our tendency to miss the panorama of our situation while we address the immediate issues at hand. For you see, I caught the flight and found a room, just as most of us have a plan to fix our errant Year 2000 programs (code). Unfortunately, I landed in the wrong state and attended a meeting in my underwear. Just as today we almost exclusively direct our Year 2000 compliance efforts toward central facilities, while ignoring the behemoth of desktops and servers collectively known as the distributed enterprise.

There is no doubt about it. The Year 2000 problem, as it applies to the distributed enterprise, is one very large and very ugly elephant. To effectively describe the care and feeding of this beast, it is prudent to first review the basics of the problem, specifically how the distributed enterprise is affected.

Before moving on, however, you are probably wondering why I would continue to dedicate a chapter to the Year 2000 in the fourth edition of this text (published in May 1999). The answer lies in the fact that there are scores of problems that will not be discovered until the turn of the century, as well as many others that will resurface after the turn of the century. For this reason, asset tracking will continue to be an essential Year 2000 remediation tool for many years to come.

SOME OLD NEW MATH

We begin this discussion with some strange mathematics. The basics of the Year 2000 problem are as simple as understanding that 00 - 48 = 52. For those of us who grew up in the computer industry during the sixties and seventies, there is a logic to this convoluted equation. Most of us, however, are stuck with Mrs. Moore's (my fourth-grade teacher) reasoning that 0 - 48 = -48. To understand how both answers can be "correct" is to understand the essence of the Year 2000 quagmire.

The above mystery math was born in the sixties when computing power was hundreds of times more expensive than it is today. The great cost of computing services caused those using them to creatively conserve these valuable resources. One such bit of ingenuity involved a particularly scarce resource called computer memory. Of equal concern in those days was the optimum use of storage (disk space). Making the most of these two scarce commodities led to some creative programming, and ultimately to our problem.

To the best of my knowledge, no one knows who came up with the trick that led to the Year 2000 problem, but I suspect his name was Waldo. I imagine Waldo working late into the night, reading stacks of computer printouts that listed column after column of dates. It was during this review that he noticed that each date had eight digits: two for the day, two for the month, and four for the year. But then his great discovery—every year on every date listed started with 19—1964, 1945, 1968, etc. "Why," Waldo mused, "should we waste valuable memory and storage on something that is always the same? Why not just calculate and store dates with the year abbreviated down to two digits (e.g., 03/04/49)?"

And so it was that Waldo, his friends, all good computer programmers, and I began to save those precious digits (bytes) by writing all our code using a two-digit-year format. It became common knowledge that December 12, 1948 and 12/12/48 were synonymous. And Waldo's trick would still be in vogue this very day if not for the change in the century. For we had written all of our programs to calculate dates with the following logic: if the year is 1971 (stored in the computer as 71), and you were born in 1948 (stored in the computer as 48) you are 71 minus 48, or 23 years old. What if, however, the year is 2000 (stored in the computer as 00), and you were born in 1948 (stored in the computer as 48)? Then, you are 00 minus 48 or -48 years old.

All of this brings us to our earlier equation, 00 - 48 = 52. When the dates are properly expressed (i.e., 2000 - 1948 = 52), the calculation makes sense. This is the essence of the Year 2000 hoopla—finding all of the old programs that use two-digit years and correcting them so they properly calculate dates into the next century.

Because of the magnitude and severity of this problem (it affects banking, accounting, and other critical applications), finding and correcting the two-digit years has spawned a whole new industry. Hundreds of companies are offering a combination of tools and personnel to assist organizations with their Year 2000 compliance problems. These contractors/consultants focus on finding and correcting programs (legacy code) that use a two-digit year.

To date, this effort has focused on identifying and correcting problems associated with centralized computing (i.e., mainframe applications). The identification and correction of errant code at the central computing facilities is a huge and complex initiative that will require substantial funding and resources. As large as this undertaking is, it may prove to be smaller, less expensive—while presenting less risk—than the Year 2000 issues that infect the distributed enterprise.

For a moment, let me ask you to imagine that you are charged with maintaining the health of a rhinoceros. Your responsibility is to inoculate the animal with numerous vaccines to prevent the onset of various diseases. Such inoculation includes identifying potentially harmful illnesses, administering the shots, periodically checking the animal to make certain that each vaccine is still effective, providing the proper dose (depending on size, age, gender, etc.), and ensuring the money is available to support the effort. This, metaphorically speaking, approximates the task of eradicating the Year 2000 problem within a centralized computing environment. To be certain, the task is not easy. Caution must be taken in the care and handling of the beast, and the medications are both expensive and complex to administer.

Now, imagine yourself performing the exact same task for 10,000 chipmunks that have free run of your enterprise. Here we discover new and more complex challenges, including: How do we find the chipmunks? How do we identify and distinguish such similar-looking creatures? How do we maintain accurate records on so many animals as they die, breed, etc.? How can we effectively plan the inoculation? How can we possibly maintain a schedule that allows us to be certain that the vaccine is still effective? How can we predict the cost of such a chaotic task? It is within this chipmunk metaphor that we discover the unique nature of eradicating Year 2000 problems across the distributed enterprise.

An asset tracking system is an essential part of managing a Year 2000 initiative across a distributed enterprise of clients and servers since an effective asset tracking system's base functionality will tell us how many chipmunks (clients and servers) we have, indicate their current condition, and report on their movements. This critical base of knowledge is the starting point of any successful compliance effort, for it is hard to imagine fixing something you can neither define nor locate. In fact, I am not aware of any means of systematically addressing the Year 2000 compliance issues across the enterprise without an effective asset tracking solution.

This knowledge alone, however, will be ineffective in addressing compliance issues unless we extend its utility. It is these extensions, along with a structured methodology, that will allow us to successfully manage the enterprise toward Year 2000 compliance.

THE PLAN

So much has been said about the complexities of the Year 2000 issue that I fear I will sound foolish when making the following statement: Enterprise management of the Year 2000 effort only requires six simple steps:

STEP	ONE:	PROBLEM IDENTIFICATION
STEP	TWO:	RISK ASSESSMENT
STEP	THREE:	RISK CORRECTION
STEP	FOUR:	COMPLIANCE PLANNING
STEP	FIVE:	COMPLIANCE MODELING
STEP	SIX:	RISK MANAGEMENT

This process allows us to understand our risks and cost-effectively manage those initiatives that economically justify correction.

The trick to this program is that you must have the necessary information (available from asset tracking), systematically execute the steps in the proper order, and continue to "loop through" the six steps well into the next century.

In my book, *Teaching Chipmunks to Dance: The Business Leaders' Guide to Making the Distributed Enterprise Year 2000 Compliant*, I address each of these steps in some detail. I encourage you to get a copy of the book as it fully explores the ties between Year 2000 compliance and the concept of asset tracking. If you'd like a copy, contact Kendall/Hunt Publishing Company in Dubuque, Iowa.

So let's see; we have an elephant under a blanket, a herd of chipmunks running amuck, all kinds of diseases, and me at a public meeting in my underwear. This is either a situation comedy, or a darned good justification for implementing an asset tracking solution.

SUMMARY

The largest things we encounter in life are not really large at all. They are but an amalgamation of tiny things that become formidable when assembled. These things are small until joined with their own kind—bricks, patriots, bacteria, votes, lies, and countless others. We must either view them en masse or lose their meaning all together.

CHAPTER 11

• ...HE SWALLOWED THE DOG •

THE PROMISE AND NONSENSE OF SYSTEMS MANAGEMENT SUITES

Me: *(Consulting with my best friend Ed about treating several sickly trees adjacent to his house)* Why would you buy topsoil for those trees when we can get it from the woods for free?

Ed: But with all the roots, it's just too hard to dig out.

Me: No, it isn't. We'll just use the soil from the giant ant mounds. It's rich, loose, and reasonably close to the house.

Ed: *(In the woods looking at the dirt mound)* It's so rich, it just seems too good to be true.

Me: *(Shoveling the first scoop into the wheelbarrow)* Get over it, Ed. Twelve loads and we can call it a day.

Ed: *(Calling me one spring morning five months later)* Chris, remember that dirt around the trees last fall?

Me: Yeah.

Ed: Two words: ants everywhere! Red ants on the trees, car, house, kids, dog, everywhere!

Me: Oops. What are you going to do about it?

Ed: I finally found some ant poison that I can use around the kids and animals. I need to saturate the earth around each tree.

Me: Gee, Ed, have you checked to make sure that it won't kill the tree?

Ed: Chris?

Me: Yes, Ed.

Ed: I'm going to kill you.

Ed and Judy Blatt are two of the really special people in my life. I would never intentionally bring harm to them, yet I found myself placing Ed in the middle of a children's song. It is a song about an old lady who swallowed a fly, and then went on to swallow various creatures in hopes of relieving the problems caused by the previous antidote. It goes: "There was an old lady who swallowed a fly...she swallowed the dog to catch the cat, she swallowed the cat to catch the bird, she swallowed the bird to catch the spider, she swallowed the spider to catch the fly, I don't know why she swallowed the fly, I guess she'll die."

Happily, the ants did not kill my friends, but they did manage to torture them for a while. And in the process of watching Ed endure the pain and expense of correcting the consequence of my bad advice, I learned a valuable lesson. Beware of ants in your topsoil.

Now the above lesson may seem to have limited utility unless you transform the elements and consider them within a broader context. In this case, the topsoil represents those actions we take to improve our control of the enterprise, while the ants represent the complexities that our actions introduce. Nowhere is this improvement/complexity dilemma more evident than in the area of systems management solutions (suites). For this reason, I have elected to address the issues surrounding these suites and how asset tracking may be the only means of keeping the ants away from the picnic of enterprise productivity.

Before introducing the ties between suites and asset tracking, it is useful to encapsulate the suite concept. Typically, suites are presented as an enterprise savior, or they are cast in league with the dark side. In the end, most thoughtful individuals neatly package them somewhere in the middle with some form of lukewarm endorsement. For instance, "These suites offer the promise of great things, yet suites are not for the faint of heart. The cost and complexity of implementation, the ongoing resource commitment, and the sheer magnitude of the undertaking make their promise anything but certain"—is typical of such an endorsement. Despite this, organizations continue to make commitments of tens of millions of dollars for systems management suites knowing that some of their corporate brethren have relegated the very same product to shelfware status.

What is it that makes these suites so attractive? Why is their promise so elusive? The answer to both of these questions is contained in a single word—complexity. For it is within the element of complexity that we discover that systems management suites exponentially increase the very problem they are designed to address. How can this be? To understand the answer, we must first isolate the core mission of suite products and examine the frustration and complexity associated with the implementation.

The balance of this chapter describes the mission and complexity of suites. It includes a disciplined and logical approach, empowering you to identify hidden implementation costs, compare the cost and requirements of competitive offerings, negotiate better terms and conditions, reduce the implementation time line, and hold vendors accountable for deliverables and time frames. At the core of this approach is asset tracking.

With an asset tracking solution, you can explore both the promise and complexity of systems management suites, such as those provided by Tivoli Systems, Computer Associates, and Hewlett-Packard. In the end, asset tracking will allow you to avoid those self-inflicted injuries that accompany the blind pursuit of a promise.

THE ELUSIVE PROMISE OF
SYSTEMS MANAGEMENT SUITES

Organizations are trying to manage a complex enterprise of clients, servers, routers, switches, and communications, as well as services that support these elements. This management includes the electronic maintenance of these components (software distribution), the management of the communications infrastructure (network management), an understanding of the current status of the various components (alert management), and the support of those using the enterprise (end-user help desk). There are many other disciplines that may be included within the definition of a systems management suite, but for the sake of simplicity, I will focus on those listed above.

Ask any competent IT professional about the complexity associated with managing any one of the above disciplines (network management, software distribution, alert management, help desk support), and you will get an earful. Each of them has the unenviable task of trying to manage and maintain a complex function across an ever-changing, geographically dispersed enterprise. Worse yet, the changes come from multiple sources (end users, server administrators, business units, etc.), and they are often neither authorized nor reported. In essence, we are asking these individuals to perform a delicate surgical procedure on a squirming patient while blindfolded.

The frustration of managing a complex task (e.g., software distribution) across an ever-changing base of assets would be impossible if it were not for the inherent interaction between these various disciplines. It is the interdependencies of these disciplines that create hope, and indeed, the promise of systems management suites.

For example, suppose those responsible for supporting end users discover that an internally developed application has a conflict with a new version of the standard corporate operating system. The help desk professional will isolate the problem and the users affected, request a fix for the application, and use the software distribution function to distribute the correction—hence the interdependence between the help desk and software distribution functions. This same type of interdependence exists within the alert and network management functions. In fact, all of the above mentioned disciplines require the others to isolate, correct, and manage problems. This of course begs the question, "Instead of using procedures and information exchange to link the various disciplines, why not purchase a single product that integrates all of these functions?" And thus, the elusive promise of systems management suites is born.

A COMPLEXITY EQUATION

With the above understanding, we can begin to visualize a complexity equation that seems to defy resolution. Successfully implementing a systems management suite requires us to simultaneously deal with three sets of variables.

First, we must deal with a continually changing enterprise (hardware, applications, configuration settings, etc.). Second, we must deal with the inherent complexity associated with each discipline (software distribution, network management, etc.). And third, we must deal with the complexity of the integration and the communication between these disciplines. It is this third element that is most often overlooked by those who are task-driven, and yet is of greatest concern to those who have experience delivering moonlandinglike missions.

Before going further, it is important to have a working knowledge of this third variable, for without this knowledge, the successful implementation of a systems management suite is impossible. Assume for a moment that we have an enterprise that is comprised of one server and one workstation connected to that server. If we were to install a software distribution application (discipline) across our enterprise, we would have to place certain code on both our client and server.

In addition, we would have to make certain that both of these elements have the proper prerequisites (operating system version, memory, free disk space, configuration settings, communication settings, etc.). Further, we would need to make certain that the newly installed system was not in conflict with our existing base of mission-critical functions. Even after this is completed, we still have to verify that the server and the workstation are communicating and delivering the proper results back to those managing the software distribution operation. This, as complex as it may seem, is a kindergartenlike task when compared to the implementation of a systems management suite.

Although the above statement may seem like hyperbole, consider the following as it is applied to our hypothetical enterprise of one server and one workstation. We are now implementing a suite that encompasses a half-dozen disciplines, each with its own set of prerequisites. In addition, these disciplines interact with one another, and the relationships between the enterprise components and the various disciplines must be established. All of this must happen while the targeted workstation and server are evolving.

Now try to imagine implementing such a suite across a geographically dispersed enterprise of 10,000 nodes, using personnel who do not have an understanding of your enterprise and/or experience implementing such a suite. Here we discover the thief that steals the promise from those purchasing suite solutions.

A SAFE PATH AROUND DISASTER

Experience tells us that as the complexity of a task increases, its returns diminish. There are many who believe that systems management suites have exceeded the complexity threshold, and that no amount of benefit can adequately compensate for the investment required to implement and maintain this complexity of complexities. Candidly, when viewing the task of implementing and managing a systems management suite as a whole, I too become discouraged. It is only when I consider the component parts of the problem that I can clearly see a safe path around certain disaster and begin to anticipate the suite's promise.

There are four major chronological blocks to the systems management suite time line: product selection, planning, implementation, and management. Interestingly, within each of these blocks, we have numerous opportunities to shoot ourselves in the foot. In reality, these self-inflicted injuries are not the result of a faulty or misrepresented product, but rather the result of our blind pursuit of a promise, without fully understanding its price. It is ignorance that loads our gun and ignorance that allows us to proceed through the systems management time line toward ever-diminishing returns.

This is not to say that perfect knowledge will, with 100 percent certainty, lead us to the full promise of a systems management suite. There are too many other factors that prevent such assurances, including the specifics of the enterprise, the talent assigned to the project, and the IT business processes that are unique to your organization. There are, however, critical pockets of knowledge that may be the measure of difference between a cost-effective implementation and a budget-busting failure.

IT IS DIFFICULT TO LEAD IF YOU ARE BLINDFOLDED

As mentioned earlier, the selection, planning, implementation, and management of a systems management suite is a complexity of complexities. Those attempting such a task must deal with three major factors: a continually changing enterprise (hardware, applications, configuration settings, etc.), the inherent complexity associated with each discipline, and the complexity of the integration and communication between the disciplines. The answer to solving this puzzle of complexity is found in the first of these factors (the continually changing enterprise).

Logic would tell us that knowledge of the distributed enterprise is the common denominator of our complexity equation. Each of the disciplines, and the joining of those disciplines into a suite, is applied against the enterprise. If we solve the enterprise uncertainty, we cancel a large number of unknowns associated with the other two variables in the equation. In other words, the key to leading an enterprise-wide selection/implementation effort is having essential information on the enterprise that you propose to change. Unfortunately, most of those undertaking the systems management suite journey lack the base of enterprise knowledge that is critical for a cost-effective implementation. Without this knowledge base, the implementation will fail, and worse yet, the organization will never understand why.

The basis for the above statement is that most organizations do not know the current state of the hardware, software, and configuration settings of the individual components that comprise their enterprise. Those who claim to have such knowledge are typically working with outdated information that was acquired via an annual physical inventory. Even those who do have some current inventory information rarely have it in a form that presents a total enterprise view, or in a form that reflects functional units (departments, divisions, geographic locations, etc.). As we shall see in the following section, lacking a current and historical understanding of how each enterprise component relates to your suite implementation effort is a definite path to disappointment, frustration, and failure.

The answer to this dilemma is the disciplined and logical approach to the selection, planning, implementation, and management of the systems management suite. At the foundation of this approach is the knowledge base provided by enterprise asset tracking technology. As described throughout this book, an effective asset tracking system automatically provides you with a current and historical view of each element in your enterprise. It allows you to view each node's configuration, and it associates that node with its function (e.g., department, division, geographic location, etc.). It creates a repository of enterprise information that is invaluable during all phases of the systems management suite initiative. The cost of such a system is typically less than 5 percent of a systems management suite, and it can be implemented across a large enterprise in a matter of weeks.

EMPOWERING THE USER

So if having an effective asset tracking system is so elemental to the successful selection and implementation of a systems management suite, why aren't companies that sell the suites eager to make asset tracking part of their proposal? The simple answer is that it is not in their best interest. A more comprehensive answer includes the fact that asset tracking information empowers users to negotiate a better deal, identifies hidden costs, facilitates accountability, and quantitatively documents the nonperforming elements of both the product and implementation effort. Why would any provider of such a complex product willingly hand their prospect the keys to such a car?

In fact, many suite vendors will tell you that there is no need for an asset tracking system, as part of their product already provides inventory information on enterprise components. There are two flaws with this logic. First, the mission-critical information that is provided by a robust asset tracking system far exceeds the minimal information that is provided by a suite's inventory component. And second, how can the inventory component of a suite assist you when its implementation is part of the problem?

In the following section, I enumerate eleven areas that can dramatically improve your chances for a successful suite implementation and substantially reduce the cost of both acquisition and implementation. These elements assume that you are empowered with an asset tracking system; however, those without such a system can also benefit from understanding these processes.

THE ELEVEN ELEMENTS OF SUCCESS

As explained earlier, there are four major chronological blocks to the systems management suite time line: product selection, planning, implementation, and management. Each of these areas presents a unique opportunity to reduce the cost and positively affect the implementation of a systems management suite. Although the format of this text prohibits me from listing all considerations, I have included the most important initiatives that can have a significantly positive impact on your systems management project.

1) DO NOT ALLOW THE SUITE VENDOR SALESPERSON TO CONTROL THE SELECTION PROCESS.

This sounds obvious; however, there are substantial forces working against you. From the get-go, suite vendors position their products as an enterprise solution with an enterprise price tag. However, you may not be able to deploy the suite in the entire enterprise. For example, does the suite support Macintosh? DOS? Older versions of NetWare? Does it support all of the current communication layers in your network? Will all nodes within your enterprise benefit from such a suite? Some applications, such as reservation systems or teller stations, may be "locked down" and only need a fraction of what is being proposed. You can take the initiative by using your asset tracking system to:

• Produce a list of servers and workstations (nodes) that are being considered for the suite.

- Obtain detailed configuration information (operating system, operating system version, machine type, etc.) on the above nodes. For example, see the following illustration.

LAST NAME	FIRST NAME	DEPT	PROCESSOR	OS
HOROWITZ	ELIZABETH	SALES	486	WIN 3.1
KROGER	SALLY	FINANCE	PENTIUM II	WIN NT
LATT	JAMES	SALES	486	WIN 3.1
SMITH	JOHN	FINANCE	PENTIUM II	WIN 95
TUCKER	ALLISON	FINANCE	PENTIUM II	WIN NT
WYNDHAM	GEORGE	SALES	386	WIN. 3.0

- Provide a list of required communication support.

Once this information is given to the vendor, ask for a written response that clearly identifies all that is supported and all that is not supported. For those items not supported, do not accept a representation of future support unless accompanied with a firm delivery date and a strong financial incentive to meet that milestone.

Oftentimes, suite vendors will dismiss configurations that they cannot support by saying that those desktops will become accessible after you complete your next technology upgrade. This may or may not be true. Many desktops run DOS, not because they are behind on the technology curve, but because it is a small footprint that optimizes a specific application. You can use your asset tracking system to help associate functions with desktops and thus avoid this pitfall.

2) Do NOT BE SEDUCED BY INCOMPLETE PRODUCT/ IMPLEMENTATION COST PROPOSALS.

The cost of the suite implementation is more than the cost of the software. Using your asset tracking system, you can specify the suite prerequisites (processor speed, operating system version, memory, disk space, communications, etc.) and model them against the targeted nodes. The result will be a list of hardware and software upgrades that must be performed to accommodate the suite, as well as a break-down of upgrade costs, including associated labor and lost productivity. The benefits of the analysis that follows are self-evident. Concisely stated, such an analysis empowers you to make an informed decision.

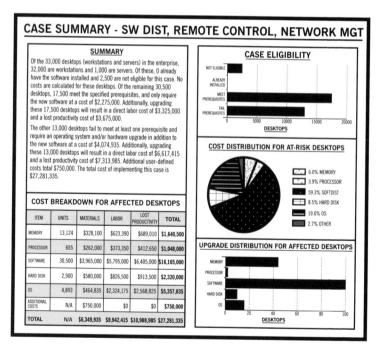

It is not unusual for the cost of prerequisite component upgrades to greatly exceed the cost of the suite license itself. Your suite provider will say, "You are always upgrading your enterprise anyway, so you really should not consider prerequisite upgrades an additional expense." I agree, as long as you are not being forced to upgrade early (there is a strong relationship between time and money), or being forced to incrementally upgrade beyond your normal plans just to accommodate the suite. As systems management suites are typically aggressive consumers of workstation and server resources, you should carefully consider this matter.

Once you have gathered the above information, summarize it to use as a basis for future discussions. Use your asset tracking system to produce a cost estimate for each component being proposed as part of the suite. In other words, how much will it cost to implement the suite's software distribution discipline across the targeted nodes? This cost would include the component fee, upgrade materials, and upgrade labor. Looking at the information contained in the analysis on the next page, you will be able to conduct a basic value-to-cost assessment. Perhaps the software distribution component is one of the least important features, and yet it represents the single largest area of expense. You may decide to eliminate it, or just as likely, confronted with the reality of your assessment, the vendor may steeply discount that component.

In addition, when modeling the upgrade requirements, do not forget to consider the known conflicts that the suite has with other applications, operating system extensions, hardware, etc. You should request a list of all known conflicts from the suite provider and consider the impact (cost and resources) of having to correct these conflicts. For more information on this topic, see point 11.

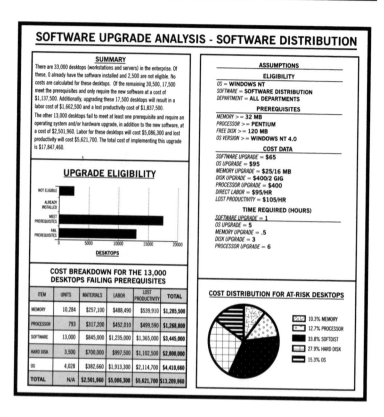

SOFTWARE UPGRADE ANALYSIS - SOFTWARE DISTRIBUTION

SUMMARY

There are 33,000 desktops (workstations and servers) in the enterprise. Of these, 0 already have the software installed and 2,500 are not eligible. No costs are calculated for these desktops. Of the remaining 30,500, 17,500 meet the prerequisites and only require the new software at a cost of $1,137,500. Additionally, upgrading these 17,500 desktops will result in a labor cost of $1,662,500 and a lost productivity cost of $1,837,500.

The other 13,000 desktops fail to meet at least one prerequisite and require an operating system and/or hardware upgrade, in addition to the new software, at a cost of $2,501,960. Labor for these desktops will cost $5,086,300 and lost productivity will cost $5,621,700. The total cost of implementing this upgrade is $17,847,460.

UPGRADE ELIGIBILITY

ASSUMPTIONS

ELIGIBILITY
OS = WINDOWS NT
SOFTWARE = SOFTWARE DISTRIBUTION
DEPARTMENT = ALL DEPARTMENTS

PREREQUISITES
MEMORY >= 32 MB
PROCESSOR >= PENTIUM
FREE DISK >= 120 MB
OS VERSION >= WINDOWS NT 4.0

COST DATA
SOFTWARE UPGRADE = $65
OS UPGRADE = $95
MEMORY UPGRADE = $25/16 MB
DISK UPGRADE = $400/2 GIG
PROCESSOR UPGRADE = $400
DIRECT LABOR = $95/HR
LOST PRODUCTIVITY = $105/HR

TIME REQUIRED (HOURS)
SOFTWARE UPGRADE = 1
OS UPGRADE = 5
MEMORY UPGRADE = .5
DISK UPGRADE = 3
PROCESSOR UPGRADE = 6

COST BREAKDOWN FOR THE 13,000 DESKTOPS FAILING PREREQUISITES

ITEM	UNITS	MATERIALS	LABOR	LOST PRODUCTIVITY	TOTAL
MEMORY	10,284	$257,100	$488,490	$539,910	$1,285,500
PROCESSOR	793	$317,200	$452,010	$499,590	$1,268,800
SOFTWARE	13,000	$845,000	$1,235,000	$1,365,000	$3,445,000
HARD DISK	3,500	$700,000	$997,500	$1,102,500	$2,800,000
OS	4,028	$382,660	$1,913,300	$2,114,700	$4,410,660
TOTAL	N/A	$2,501,960	$5,086,300	$5,621,700	$13,209,960

COST DISTRIBUTION FOR AT-RISK DESKTOPS

- 10.3% MEMORY
- 12.7% PROCESSOR
- 33.8% SOFTDIST
- 27.9% HARD DISK
- 15.3% OS

3) ASK FOR A FIXED-PRICE BID FOR SUCCESSFUL ROLLOUT.

Suite providers, and their associated consulting/implementation arms, fully understand the difficulty and risks associated with implementing this complexity of complexities. In the past, smart IT executives (without the benefit of asset tracking information) tried to mitigate their risks by requesting a fixed-price bid on the implementation of the suite offering. The suite provider, in almost all cases, declined, indicating that "uncertainties within the enterprise" presented unacceptable levels of risk.

With the information available from an asset tracking system, these same suite vendors are now confronted with all the information required to enter into a fixed-price implementation agreement. You, via your asset tracking system, are able to provide vendors with detailed information (see the following report) on every targeted desktop, including user, location, and required upgrades.

USER LAST NAME	USER FIRST NAME	USER DEPARTMENT	USER WORK ADDRESS	USER WORK CITY	CURRENT RAM	REQUIRED RAM
Aba-haloum	Gordon	Administration	31 5th St.	Raleigh	12288	16 MB
Abel	Diane	Finance	31 5th St.	Raleigh	16384	0
Adams	Jennifer	Marketing	31 5th St.	Raleigh	4096	16 MB
Agostino	Grace	Administration	31 5th St.	Raleigh	8192	16 MB
Alter	Carolyn	Administration	31 5th St.	Raleigh	8192	16 MB
Appleman	Ronald	IT	31 5th St.	Raleigh	4096	16 MB
Asher	Rebecca	IT	31 5th St.	Raleigh	8192	16 MB
Austed	Benjamin	IT	31 5th St.	Raleigh	16384	0
Barnes	Mike	Service	31 5th St.	Raleigh	4096	16 MB
Basile	Janet	IT	31 5th St.	Raleigh	4096	16 MB
Bauchman	Edward	Marketing	31 5th St.	Raleigh	16384	0
Beaubien	Kathy	IT	31 5th St.	Raleigh	8192	16 MB

With this information, you can challenge many of the claims vendors make about how easy your systems management suite will be to implement. Should the vendor, even with the above information, still refuse to consider a fixed-price bid, then you should aggressively explore his reasons for doing so. Should the fixed-price bid come in excessively high, you should be equally aggressive in your investigation. If the bid is acceptably low, and assuming the license fees are also tied to implementation, you are in a position to enter into a partnership in which the risks are shared.

None of this is to suggest that you should only consider the suite provider for implementation services. There are many capable firms that provide implementation assistance. Regardless of whom you select to deploy the suite (internal or external), it is wise to ask the suite provider for a fixed-price implementation bid. Seeing how they fence in their risks educates you on the limitations and requirements of implementing the suite.

4) DO NOT FOCUS TOO EARLY ON A SINGLE SUITE PROVIDER.

Regardless of your prejudices, you should continue an active dialog with at least two or three providers throughout the entire selection process. Your thorough analysis may alter your earlier selection as deficiencies in the areas of cost, network support, prerequisites, and platform support are exposed. In addition, having detailed information on cost and technical requirements allows you to leverage the low-cost vendor against a more desirable provider.

5) DO NOT FALL INTO THE TRAP OF TESTING A SYSTEMS MANAGEMENT SUITE IN A LAB ENVIRONMENT.

The types of systems management suites that are available are too active and too configuration-dependent to make testing them in a laboratory environment reliable. In addition, much of what these suites undertake is hardware intensive, and thus the suite must be stressed beyond controlled limits to ascertain its viability. Therefore, should a vendor assure you that the suite has been fully tested, do not assume the suite is necessarily capable of meeting your needs.

6) DO NOT FALL INTO THE "REFERENCE TEST" TRAP.

In this case, you are given a reference for every feature that you are interested in as an assurance of the product's viability. Reference tests almost always prove ineffective when it comes to suite evaluations because networks differ, volumes differ, and the real test of a suite is its ability to integrate all of its functions across your enterprise. It is unlikely that five different references testifying to a half-dozen features will give you the assurances that you require.

7) EXPECT BREAKAGE AND REPAIR EXPENSES.

A functioning enterprise is fragile. Over the years mission-critical systems acquire multiple layers of enhancements and fixes that are configuration-dependent. In addition, end users and departments acquire configuration-dependent tools that silently become part of their mission-critical operation. To a greater or lesser extent, all of these systems will be affected by the implementation of a systems management suite.

As described earlier, a deployed suite may require the memory, processor, hard disk, and communications devices to be upgraded, or it may merely require the installation of its own software. In any case, the desktop will undergo substantial modifications. Within this swirl of change, applications that have functioned for years may begin to behave erratically or cease working. Troubleshooting such conditions is especially expensive as the knowledge base required to unravel the problem includes both an understanding of the modules installed as part of the suite, as well as an understanding of the mission-critical application base.

The repository supplied by an effective asset tracking system can be especially valuable in stabilizing affected workstations and servers. Because the repository contains both current and previous views of the hardware and software configuration of each workstation and server, those troubleshooting can view each node before and after each phase of the implementation. This greatly reduces the time it takes to identify conflicts and, if necessary, allows you to return the desktop to its original (working) state.

Beware, even if you are not required to modify the desktop hardware, you are still making substantial changes when installing a suite. The agents placed on the desktop as part of a suite deployment must be active if they are to accomplish their assigned tasks. These active agents interact with the operating system and with each other as they perform and monitor a complex series of activities. You should, as part of your evaluation, understand the function and impact that each agent may have on mission-critical systems.

Needless to say, before beginning the implementation, you should allow the proper time and resources for troubleshooting. This must include personnel who are intimately familiar with your mission-critical applications and thoroughly versed in the suite product.

8) ASK TO PAY AS YOU GO.

Success stories on the full implementation of a systems management suite across a reasonably large enterprise are rare. Those stories we do hear about, upon investigation, generally involve either a very small number of nodes, or the implementation of only a small portion of the suite offering. I recently read an article that purported to be a strong endorsement of systems management suites. I was not surprised to read the references lament again and again about the high cost and slow pace of implementation. The customer in this case did achieve an enterprise rollout. The real punch line came late in the article when it was disclosed that the customer had only implemented a single feature of the suite (enterprise alerts).

I am never surprised at the cost and pace of implementing a suite; after all, it is a complexity of complexities. I am, however, always surprised at the terms under which the suites are procured. In the majority of cases, the customer is sold an enterprise license for the entire product suite. Regardless of the "deal" you are being offered, this makes little or no sense. Consider asking for a pay-as-you-go purchasing agreement and do the following:

- Use your asset tracking repository to isolate a representative portion of your enterprise. A functional unit (marketing, finance, etc.) is often a good selection because it offers a cross-section of node types and a representative sample of your network. Ideally, this should represent at least 5 percent of your enterprise.

- Select the first feature of the suite that you wish to deploy (software distribution, alerts, network management, etc.). Procure the necessary software and deployment resources and implement the first feature on the targeted nodes. Using your asset repository, keep accurate records of required resources, problems encountered, and elapsed time to complete the effort.

- If the above effort is acceptable and you wish to move forward, select the next portion of the suite and install it on the same targeted nodes. Again, note the time, resources, and problems encountered in the effort. Continue this process until you have implemented (or attempted to implement) all portions of the suite that are of interest.

- Assess the fully loaded cost (software, upgrade, labor, reengineering, etc.) of each component installed. Compare the fully loaded cost to the perceived benefit and select those components that are viable for your enterprise.

- Now you are ready to negotiate an enterprise license for those components that make sense for your enterprise. After you have negotiated your best deal, ask the vendor to retroactively give you the same price for the nodes you already purchased.

This method has several advantages. It prevents you from buying an enterprise license for a product or component that you cannot afford to install. It allows you to negotiate for the specific types of support that you will require during the enterprise rollout. It prevents you from purchasing a product that does not meet your requirements. And it allows you to enter into this ambitious undertaking fully knowledgeable of both the costs and risks.

9) MINIMIZE MULTIPLE VISITS TO THE WORKSTATIONS AND SERVERS.

Perhaps the greatest benefit of having an asset tracking repository underneath your suite implementation effort is asset tracking's ability to minimize desktop visits. With a complete understanding of the required upgrades, conflicts, and configuration settings broken down by desktop, you can greatly reduce the number of desktop visits required to implement the suite. Do not underestimate the importance of this area because desktop implementation is almost always the single largest area of expense associated with a suite implementation.

The most effective format for such asset tracking information is a work order (see the example on the next page). Information in this format allows you to manage each desktop visit and verify the results of that visit.

10) MAINTAIN PROACTIVE CONTROL OF THE IMPLEMENTATION.

The implementation of a systems management suite can be frustrating and confusing. If you contract to have the suite installed on all or part of your enterprise, how do you know when it is accomplished? How are you certain that the milestones are being met? What workstations and servers only have a partial installation? Which nodes have been overlooked? Which nodes have removed the application?

WORK ORDER - SYSFRAME
CREATED 3/15/1998 10:41 A.M.

USER LAST NAME -	**SMITH**
USER FIRST NAME -	**JOHN**
USER JOB TITLE -	**CHIEF FINANCIAL OFFICER**
USER DEPARTMENT -	**FINANCE**
USER WORK ADDRESS -	**PEACHTREE CORP. BLDG**
	1111 SILICON CENTER DRIVE
USER WORK CITY -	**ATLANTA**
USER WORK STATE -	**GEORGIA**
USER WORK ZIP -	**30076**
USER PHONE NUMBER -	**(770) 851-1234**
USER PHONE EXTENSION -	**848**
UNIQUE IDENTIFIER -	**254386D**

DESKTOP CONFIGURATION - 3/13/1998 3:03 P.M.

SYSTEM	CURRENT	REQUIRED UPGRADE
PROCESSOR	**486**	**PENTIUM**
MEMORY	**8 MB**	**+16 MB**
DISK CAPACITY	**1250 MB**	**N/A**
OPERATING SYSTEM	**WIN 95**	**WIN NT**

SOFTWARE PRODUCT	CURRENT	REQUIRED VERSION
SYSFRAME SOFTDIST	**N/A**	**VERSION 5.0**
SYSFRAME REMOTECONT	**N/A**	**VERSION 5.0**
SYSFRAME NETWORKMGT	**N/A**	**VERSION 5.0**

PERFORMED BY:_____**COMPLETED:**_____

Keeping in mind that the implementation of a full suite may span years in a large enterprise, it is wise to benchmark the suite rollout against the asset tracking repository. Using both the current and historical information contained in the repository, portions of the enterprise can be targeted for deployment, the status of deployment can be monitored, and trends (projections) can be extrapolated. Such analysis of the enterprise allows for the proactive management of both the suite provider and those implementing the application. Having repository information available to assist you in monitoring implementation progress allows you to fully leverage performance penalty clauses that you negotiate into your contracts.

11) AVOID SUITE FAILURE.

The best of suite products, perfectly implemented, will cease to function on some percent of the enterprise. In most cases, this failure has nothing to do with the suite application, but rather is due to the changes initiated at the workstation or server. Such changes include the installation of a new product, an upgrade or patch to the operating system, or a user-inspired change to the configuration. These changes, if not proactively managed, erode the implementation effort and/or the effectiveness of the deployed suite. Secondarily, as large blocks of users fail to realize the value of the suite promise, the confidence in both the product and those implementing it continues to erode.

Fortunately, the knowledge and tools required to avoid this situation are readily available. The suite provider should be required to provide a list of the prerequisites for each node configuration in the enterprise. In addition, you should request a list of all known conflicts that the suite has with other applications, operating system extensions, hardware, etc. Armed with the above information, you can create conditions that your asset tracking repository can flag as they are encountered. Specifically, as the asset tracking system gathers its latest image of each workstation and server within the enterprise, it compares the image against the required prerequisites and the known areas of conflict. The tracking system then sends a signal informing the proper party that a condition which may prohibit the suite from functioning properly has been identified. Note that the modeling of conflicts can also be invaluable when choosing a suite offering. For more information, see point 2.

THE UNPOPULAR TRUTH

I do not expect this chapter to make me very popular with those who sell systems management suites. The above elements surely will slow down their sales cycle as you pursue an implementation plan in phases. It will reduce revenues as you purchase only those products that you need and are capable of implementing. It will drive down consulting margins as you are empowered with the knowledge to seek and evaluate competitive implementation bids. It will require both product and service providers to assign better resources to your account as you are empowered with the knowledge to hold them accountable for the deliverables negotiated in the contract. And it will reduce the cost of the product being proposed as you understand the full implications of implementing your system and evaluating competitive products.

And as you thrash through the denials and protests that suite vendors direct at the above concepts, I would encourage you to ask yourself the following questions: "Why are these folks so hostile toward such an obviously logical process? Has their zeal for the sale overtaken their interest in my success? Why are they afraid of my empowerment?" These are not questions I can answer, but they are issues that are in your best interest to consider. Best of luck with your systems management effort.

SUMMARY

Even angels dancing on the head of a pin avoid juggling eggs while doing so.

CHAPTER 12

CHANNEL 23

MOVES, ADDS, AND CHANGES

Me: *(To my wife Judi)* The cable company has rearranged the channels again.

Judi: That's the third time in the past six months. Why do they keep doing it?

Me: I have no idea, but I can't find ABC.

Cable Company Operator: *(Via phone)* Customer Service, how may I help you?

Me: I can't find ABC on my cable service.

Cable Company Operator: Frequently we temporarily lose some of our programming when we reassign channels.

Me: Have you checked underneath the couch cushions?

Cable Company Operator: I'm sorry?

Me: I don't mean to be flip, but you've rearranged the channels three times in just six months and every time it seems to cause problems.

Cable Company Operator: Sir, rearranging the channels makes us more efficient.

Me: I don't understand. How does scrambling the channels every two months make you more efficient?

Cable Company Operator: I'm sorry sir, but I'm only a temporary employee hired to help handle peak customer service traffic. I can give you the number for the business office.

Me: So you only really work when the company's flooded with complaints because of channel reassignments?

Cable Company Operator: Yes sir, we double our response lines to maintain a consistent level of service.

Me: I have to go now. You're making my brain hurt.

Although to this day I cannot fathom how rearranging channels makes a cable company more efficient, I have accepted it as some form of complex, obtuse truth. I fully believe that somehow ABC operates more efficiently on channel 23 than it did on channel 13. Further, I know that we, the viewing public, are better off for suffering the disorientation of this semimonthly channel-scrambling ritual, and that the newspapers and *TV Guide* relish the expense of keeping up with this folly. I believe, I believe, but in spite of this profound insight, two words keep coursing through my thoughts—"deregulate cable."

How easy it is for us to look upon the actions of the cable company as some form of moronic self-induced malady brought on by the lack of competition, but in truth we all suffer regularly from the same disease. This ailment I speak of is not about the changes that we make, but about the costs that we fail to associate with our alterations. Simply stated, every time we move, add, or change one of our life's assets/missions, we pay a price. This applies to cars, homes, spouses, stocks, and careers. And at this point in the text, there should be no surprise that it especially applies to the distributed enterprise.

Thus far, this book has focused on the business aspect of understanding the makeup of the enterprise and its speed and direction of change. This chapter, although reinforcing these concepts, focuses on the subject of change and how change is measured by an effective asset tracking system. For change is a major cost and dynamic of any mission, and if we are to succeed it must be tracked, related, and recognized as part of the overall mission. Or, in keeping with our analogy, we will discover how to put the cable viewer into direct contact with those making the decision to reassign the channels.

A DISCUSSION OF CHANGE

Within the IT industry, enterprise evolution is generally referred to as "Move Add Change." This, of course, begs the question, "Isn't moving something or adding something a change?" The obvious answer is yes; however, the word "change" has such a variety of meanings and so few synonyms that it invites word confusion. It is for this reason that I will define precise terms as they relate to specific aspects of change. It is my hope that in strictly sticking to these definitions during the balance of this chapter, I might bring us to a common understanding of the concept of enterprise change management, a.k.a. Move Add Change.

DEFINITIONS

CHANGE ELEMENT

A Change Element is the lowest or most basic level of change. Each time a component of a desktop or server is modified, an element of change is introduced into the distributed enterprise. The addition of a disk drive, the upgrade of an operating system, the installation of a game, or connectivity to a new server are all Change Elements. In reality, there are hundreds of different types of changes that may be associated with enterprise processors. Many of these elements are harmless as they have little associated costs and no impact on either the user or the enterprise. Other Change Elements, however, carry substantial costs and both directly and indirectly impact the end user, the enterprise, and the mission of the organization.

QUALIFIED CHANGE

A Qualified Change is any modification, introduction, or removal of an enterprise asset that is of sufficient magnitude to deserve consideration. *Note: A Qualified Change may be made up of multiple Change Elements.* Identifying (qualifying) a Change Element as being significant or meaningful is a human process. For example, we may know that each time we add a disk drive to a desktop, the end user loses four hours of productivity ($420), we incur four hours of contract labor expense to install the device ($380), and we pay for equipment ($400). This $1,200, along with the associated disruption, may lead us to consider it an important change, i.e., a change significant enough to be considered.

There are Change Elements that are not important when considered alone, but when joined in certain combinations become qualified. A straightforward example of this complexity is our desire to know when a desktop is physically relocated within the enterprise. Clearly, one way to discover relocation is to have those moving the desktop report the change to the asset tracking system. On the other hand, suppose that the movement of the device was not reported due to an oversight or even willful negligence. Without the support of those relocating the device, is it still possible to detect its movement?

Yes, with an effective asset tracking solution. By using qualification criteria, the asset tracking system can discover and join various Change Elements and flag this combination as a Qualified Change. For instance, the asset tracking system automatically tracks desktop configurations, including changes to the desktop's TCP/IP address, gateway address, server address, network address, and department. Any one of these changes may not indicate that the desktop has been moved, but we can logically identify combinations of changes that indicate a physical relocation has occurred with a high degree of certainty. In this example, we may decide that the combination of an IP address and network address change is sufficient to identify the desktop as having moved. Here we have joined Change Elements to define a Qualified Change.

ENTERPRISE MOVE ADD CHANGE

An Enterprise Move Add Change is the quantification and association of Qualified Change activity with the organization's business and management objectives. This is a logical component of an effective asset tracking solution.

WHO CARES?

Before moving on to the more tedious aspects of change, it is useful to delineate those who will gain the greatest benefit from understanding Enterprise Move Add Change and proactively associating change with mission. This summary is general in nature, dealing in large organization blocks and sweeping categories of application. It is not intended to be a road map of specific utility, but rather an illustration of what is possible.

IT MANAGEMENT

Someone (usually the IT department) within every organization must ensure the stability of the distributed enterprise. There are many aspects to this mission, including selecting correct equipment and software, ensuring adequate communications facilities, and providing a range of support services. Ultimately, however, these aspects are merely dancers performing part of a complex ballet of change. The continuing upgrade and addition of desktops, new software, enhanced connectivity, and evolving missions make change a constant. Further complicating this production is the fact that much of this change is unauthorized.

Clearly, those responsible for enterprise stability have a need to relate both the amount and the distribution of change to the business and enterprise mission. As we shall see, the secret to accomplishing this lies not in the details, but in a strategic analysis of a complex choreography that is only understood when bound within a specific time period.

FUNCTIONAL MANAGEMENT

It may at first seem odd that understanding the amount and type of change within the distributed enterprise could be of value in managing business functions, but knowledge of enterprise change may indeed be mission critical.

For example, if you are responsible for the productivity of bank tellers and you discover that their desktops are continually undergoing numerous software changes, do you care? Of course you do, for the teller station is your gateway to productivity, and excessive change is an indicator of either continuing problems or unauthorized use. In either case, relating these changes to teller productivity can, over time, allow you to isolate and address productivity issues.

Additional examples of functional management productivity gains are covered later in this chapter.

ASSET MANAGEMENT

The value of understanding change is obvious in this case. If your mission is optimizing the return on assets, and you learn that during the previous period 800 desktops were added to the enterprise, fifty desktops were retired, and only thirty-five new employees joined the company, would you have a question? Of course you would, but only if the new and retired desktop information were presented comparatively. An effective asset tracking system not only contains such information, but also presents it in a format that makes it meaningful across all business disciplines.

COST MANAGEMENT

Those charged with managing expenses are often ignorant of the factors that generate the costs. Nowhere is this more true than in managing change across the distributed enterprise. For example, would those managing the cost side of the change equation be more effective in their research and vendor negotiations if they knew that the organization spent twice as much relocating desktops as they did procuring new devices?

The epiphanies of cost management come from understanding the relationships among alternatives. Understanding alternatives comes from grasping their proportional relationships. An effective asset tracking system presents these broad relationships so we can discover the Holy Grail of cost management—improved service through reduced cost.

FACILITIES MANAGEMENT

Perhaps the most direct application of Enterprise Move Add Change is found in organizations that outsource the care and management of their distributed enterprise to a third party. Sometimes this arrangement requires the service provider to purchase the assets that make up the distributed enterprise and assume total control of their operation. In other cases, the service provider simply delivers specified services and maintains the enterprise to a defined standard. In between these two extremes are countless variations. In any case, understanding Enterprise Move Add Change is central to the success of both parties.

From the organization's perspective, an effective asset tracking system allows it to negotiate a better contract and track the performance of the service provider. By understanding both how the enterprise is constructed and how it evolves, the organization can outsource areas of its enterprise that are troublesome, keeping only those that can effectively be managed internally. For example, an organization may be fully confident that it can replace desktops at the end of their useful life, but the organization may believe it is incapable of maintaining desktops in a production environment.

Enterprise Move Add Change is of equal interest to service providers because they are contractually bound to provide specific service levels and, in most cases, have the opportunity to increase their fee if the number of enterprise changes exceeds a certain threshold. In this case, accurate records can mean the difference between a profitable contract and a financial disaster. It is imperative that service providers understand the base of assets for which they are assuming responsibility, as well as the volume of change that is occurring for each billing period.

Within facilities management, both parties benefit from the deliverables of an asset tracking system. The organization contracting for services is not put in a position of having the fox watch the henhouse, while the service provider does not suffer heavy losses because of mistakenly underestimating changes. Here both parties use the exact same information to protect their individual best interests.

UNDERSTANDING THE BEAST

Within every world there is a beast dominating the landscape. Inside the world of Enterprise Move Add Change that creature is the end user. It is the end user who either causes or is the recipient of all change that is associated with the distributed enterprise. It is therefore logical that any rational discussion of enterprise change must begin with and be inseparably tied to the end user.

When we associate change with the end user, we begin to understand the magnitude of the problem. There are new users requiring new desktops, users who transfer and inherit existing desktops, users who have their existing desktops retired and receive a replacement, users who have their desktops upgraded with additional hardware and/or software, and users who relocate and take their desktops with them. As discussed earlier in this chapter, all of these activities have three potential cost components—the cost of the hardware and software, the cost of end-user lost productivity, and the cost of labor for those implementing the change.

It is the cost aspect of end-user change that ties together the interests of those who manage the enterprise with those who use it as a means to an end. Both of these factions, if they are to proactively manage their responsibilities, must at some level be concerned about the productivity and the cost of maintaining the knowledge unit.

The beginning of any such exercise is using the asset tracking system to generate an Enterprise Change Analysis. Such an analysis is comprised of six sections, each of which gives the reader insight into how change is impacting both enterprise costs and the functions (departments, divisions, etc.) that make up the organization.

ENTERPRISE CHANGE ANALYSIS

The first step in preparing an Enterprise Change Analysis is to associate a cost with each predefined Qualified Change. For example, the cost of deploying a new desktop would include hardware, software, shipping, installation, loss of end-user productivity, incremental communication, etc. Along with similar estimates for other Qualified Changes, this estimate is then used to generate an analysis that highlights the strategic cost and impact of enterprise change. Because these cost estimates are used as part of a high-level analysis, it is not critical that they be absolutely precise. An accuracy level of plus or minus 10 percent will generate acceptable estimates that can be refined as the system generates an improved understanding of enterprise change. I highly recommend that a central authority establish and maintain these cost standards. Consistency of cost standards is quintessential to producing consistent and actionable results.

Once a corporate cost standard has been associated with each Qualified Change, those requesting the analysis need only define the Qualified Changes that are to be evaluated. When this is complete, the asset tracking system searches the historical asset repository for Qualified Changes and generates a single-page analysis highlighting six aspects of the "change equation" as shown in the example below.

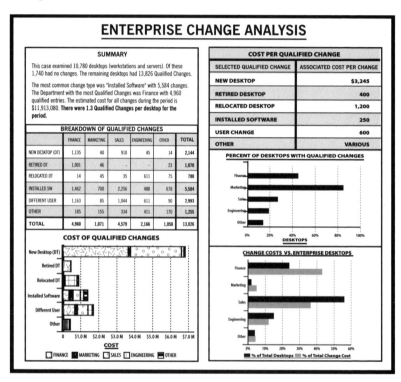

Enterprise change analysis — cost per qualified change

We begin the detailed review of this analysis by first looking at Section 4. It is a summary of costs incurred to implement each Qualified Change. The person running this report has selected (from a pull-down list) the Qualified Changes to be included in the analysis and the predefined cost that is associated with each change as shown in Section 4 on the next page.

COST PER QUALIFIED CHANGE	
SELECTED QUALIFIED CHANGE	ASSOCIATED COST PER CHANGE
NEW DESKTOP	$3,245
RETIRED DESKTOP	400
RELOCATED DESKTOP	1,200
INSTALLED SOFTWARE	250
DIFFERENT USER	600
OTHER	VARIOUS

Each time I present the above chart as an example, I become engaged in a discussion of whether these costs are high or low. In my opinion, they are conservative cost estimates. When considering the Qualified Change "New Desktop," I included $2,500 for the cost of equipment and software, three hours of downtime for the user receiving the new device ($315), three hours of support time for those installing the new system ($285), one hour of incremental help desk support ($95) and travel/misc. expense ($50). In this case, I assumed a fully loaded labor rate of $95 and a lost productivity rate of $105. As the other estimates follow a similar pattern, I will refrain from reviewing them in detail. *Note: To assist the reader in constructing the costs associated with various Qualified Change elements, I have prepared an Enterprise Change Worksheet. Refer to page 207 to request a copy of this document.*

Of special note in the above table is the Qualified Change entitled "Different User." This highlights the fact that there needs to be a robust base of discovery technology feeding the asset tracking repository to detect this type of change. For example, one of the ways you can determine if there is a new user permanently assigned to a desktop is to discover a change in the e-mail user ID. Without this discovery technology, it is unlikely that an accurate record of desktop user changes could be obtained.

Note: I have also prepared an Evaluation Checklist that provides a summary of essential discovery elements. See page 207 to request a copy of this document.

ENTERPRISE CHANGE ANALYSIS — SUMMARY

Using the information contained in Section 4, an analysis is generated that begins with a Summary (Section 1). The Summary provides the strategic framework for understanding the other sections of the report. It may be the only portion of the analysis used by certain high-level managers. For example, a CIO may have recently joined a company that has a very unstable distributed enterprise. Knowing that change is destabilizing and that dozens of different programs may be responsible, she establishes a strategic goal of reducing the number of Qualified Changes to .5 changes per desktop per period. Such a goal forces her to consider change reduction as part of every program that the company touches, and the Summary empowers her to evaluate their efforts for the period.

SUMMARY

This case examined 10,780 desktops (workstations and servers). Of these 1,740 had no changes. The remaining desktops had 13,826 Qualified Changes.

The most common change type was "Installed Software" with 5,584 changes. The Department with the most Qualified Changes was Finance with 4,960 qualified entries. The estimated cost for all changes during the period is $11,913,080. **There were 1.3 Qualified Changes per desktop for the period.**

The power of a global metric (e.g., Qualified Changes per desktop) should not be underestimated. Global metrics can be a thermometer placed under the enterprise's tongue, telling those responsible about the general condition of the patient. Global metrics allow us to establish mission goals that give direction to the countless programs that get lost in the everyday grind of operations. They tell us what is important and where we might look to find our ills. In the above example, the Summary provides our CIO with a simple metric that charts progress and keeps her subordinates mission-oriented.

ENTERPRISE CHANGE ANALYSIS – BREAKDOWN OF QUALIFIED CHANGES

Section 2 of the analysis takes us from the macro to the micro. It tabulates changes by type across functional units (departments). At first a numeric table may appear to be the least interesting element of the analysis; however, its dual purpose makes it indispensable. Its first purpose is to provide a baseline for analyzing other elements of the analysis. For example, if you learned from one of the analysis graphs that 40 percent of the desktops in finance had experienced at least one Qualified Change during the reporting period, you would likely want to know what type of change contributed to the statistic. The second purpose of this section is to give us insight into the relationships among various Qualified Changes.

BREAKDOWN OF QUALIFIED CHANGES						
	FINANCE	MARKETING	SALES	ENGINEERING	OTHER	**TOTAL**
NEW DESKTOP (DT)	1,135	40	910	45	14	**2,144**
RETIRED DT	1,001	46	-	-	23	**1,070**
RELOCATED DT	14	45	35	611	75	**780**
INSTALLED SW	1,462	700	2,256	488	678	**5,584**
DIFFERENT USER	1,163	85	1,044	611	90	**2,993**
OTHER	185	155	334	411	170	**1,255**
TOTAL	**4,960**	**1,071**	**4,579**	**2,166**	**1,050**	**13,826**

There are numerous questions that deserve consideration when examining the above table, but I have elected to highlight an anomaly within engineering. The engineering column reports forty-five new desktops, 611 relocated devices, and 611 desktops with a different user. Upon investigation, we may find a valid reason for this activity, but more likely we will discover the common practice of cascading desktops.

Cascading is the practice of assigning the most powerful machine to the most senior employee and passing down older desktops until a seniority/power equilibrium is reached across the whole department. This is especially prevalent within technical organizations. In this case, because newer machines are more powerful, the top forty-five technicians in the department received the new devices. They in turn passed their devices down to the next level, and so on. Cascading, although obviously inefficient, is a common practice within many organizations.

Section 2 provides the quantitative information in a format that allows us to consider the relationships among various types of change.

ENTERPRISE CHANGE ANALYSIS – COST OF QUALIFIED CHANGES

The next section of the analysis (Section 3) equalizes these quantities

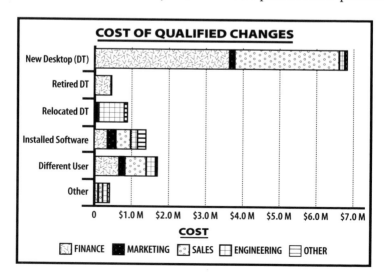

by translating them into dollars.

Converting the number of changes into dollars and graphically displaying the results gives us a new understanding of the impact of each change. There are numerous insights that can be gleaned from this chart; however, three are most prominent.

1) Our earlier observation about the reassigned (cascading) desktops in engineering now has a cost associated with it. Looking at the third bar from the top, we discover just under $1 million of cost is tied to Relocated Desktops with the vast majority incurred by engineering.

2) Looking at the top bar, we discover that the largest Qualified Change expense for the period was New Desktops, reaching nearly $7 million.

3) Examining the top two bars, we discover that sales, although spending significant money on new desktops, incurred no expense in retired desktops. This may prompt a call to the personnel department to determine the number of incremental employees added to sales during the period.

The breakdown provided in Section 3 of the analysis can be invaluable in establishing relationships among change, mission, and waste. There is, however, another aspect of change that it fails to address—the impact of disruption.

Each time we change a desktop we disrupt the user. This disruption takes end users away from their primary task, creating inefficiency within their respective work unit. Those responsible for managing change across the distributed enterprise understand that there is a threshold of change; if exceeded, the change begins to impact the mission of a functional area. In this case, it is the saturation, rather than the volume, of change that is significant.

ENTERPRISE CHANGE ANALYSIS –
PERCENT OF DESKTOPS WITH QUALIFIED CHANGES

Section 5 of the analysis provides a means for measuring change saturation across various business functions.

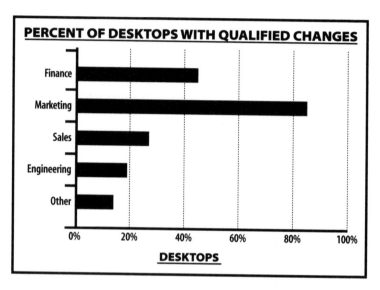

Section 5 plots the percentage of desktops that had Qualified Changes within each department. For example, we see that 85 percent of all desktops within marketing experienced at least one Qualified Change during the period. With this new perspective, marketing has gone from being one of the least visible departments (based on volume and cost considerations) to being the department most affected by change.

An interesting relationship between finance and sales is also revealed when the saturation of change is considered. Again, during our consideration of volume and cost, these two departments appeared to be experiencing an equal amount of change. Proportionately, however, finance has absorbed almost twice as much change as sales.

The information provided in this section can be used in a variety of ways. In organizations where desktop autonomy exists within business functions, the information can be used to educate the functional leaders of self-inflicted inefficiencies. Such information can also be used to explain a temporary decline in enterprise stability for a specific organization, or if run frequently enough, it can be used to allocate support services. In this example, perhaps the most important thing it tells us is to do everything we can to slow down the pace of change in both marketing and finance. It is in everyone's best interest to stabilize their technology base before undertaking any additional aggressive change initiatives.

ENTERPRISE CHANGE ANALYSIS –
CHANGE COSTS VS. ENTERPRISE DESKTOPS

The final section of the analysis, Section 6 (see next page), provides a comparative anchor that allows us to view the cost of change within the context of the business enterprise. In this case, the anchor is the number of desktops within a department expressed as a percentage of total desktops within the organization. This anchor is then associated with the total cost of Qualified Changes for each department and expressed as a percentage of total cost of Qualified Changes for the enterprise. More simply stated, the graph says to each department, "You are this big, and you are eating this much of our change expense pie."

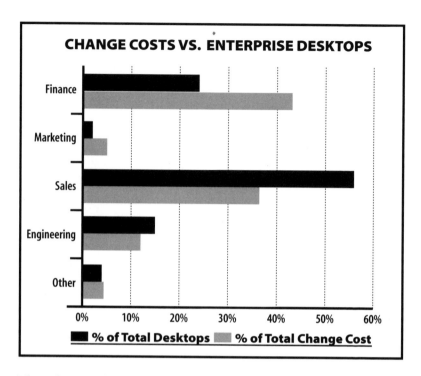

CHANGE COSTS VS. ENTERPRISE DESKTOPS

■ % of Total Desktops   ▓ % of Total Change Cost

This chart isolates those functional areas that are consuming a disproportionate percentage of the Qualified Change expenditures. In the above example, finance, although only representing 24 percent of the desktops within the enterprise, is consuming 43 percent of Qualified Change expenditures. Marketing is spending more than twice its fair share, while sales and engineering are relatively modest in their consumption.

Ideally, those managing change across the distributed enterprise should be able to predict the comparative percentages for each department before running the analysis. Perhaps finance is in the middle of a long-planned technology refresh, and marketing has a scheduled upgrade of its office suite. In the real world, however, many changes occur with no prior knowledge and go undetected unless reported by an effective asset tracking system. It is within this section of the analysis that those charged with tracking some form of total cost of ownership gain a critical advantage. For when you are empowered with the knowledge of what was planned, and you are presented with a quantitative analysis of the depth and location of various types of change, the management of Enterprise Move Add Change becomes a reality.

HOW MUCH IS ENOUGH?

Any discussion of the Enterprise Change Analysis inevitably leads to a question of frequency. How often should such an analysis be run and what period of time should it cover? The answer to this question is partly dependent on your enterprise and your business. In general, however, I consider it prudent to run the above analysis for the current period and continue to do so monthly and quarterly. The current period in this case relates to how often you take snapshots of the enterprise. (For the purposes of this discussion, I have assumed a current period to be two weeks.)

Running the Enterprise Change Analysis for the current period (i.e., the past two weeks) allows you to discover emerging activity and rectify potential problems before they occur. You may discover a cascading of desktops or a department's unauthorized upgrade of an operating system. By focusing the analysis on a short period of time, you highlight spikes that give you an early warning of undesirable activity.

The monthly window of the Enterprise Change Analysis gives those evaluating change a means of establishing both a uniform point of comparison and a connection to the operational budget cycle. By generating analyses that mirror budget variance reports, enterprise change becomes a real component of financial management.

Quarterly reporting has the advantage of smoothing out short-term anomalies and matching up with financial reporting windows. It allows senior managers to get a feel for how excessive or unauthorized change may have impacted quarterly financial performance.

Quarterly reporting also has the advantage of accumulating cost numbers that are of a sufficient magnitude to get the attention of senior management.

PIECES AND PARTS

Thus far, I have focused on a single analysis as a means of highlighting the methodology and benefits derived from an asset tracking system's Enterprise Move Add Change component. There are, however, other aspects of an asset tracking solution that must be in place to effectively manage change.

Within the context of asset tracking, Enterprise Move Add Change begins with automatically and transparently discovering the changes that occurred in the desktop population. Certain pieces of information are disproportionately important when using an asset tracking solution to manage change. These elements include:

Change in E-mail Address	Change in Employee ID or Name
Work Group User Change	Network Login Change
Department Change	IP Address Change
Gateway Change	Changed LAN Board

This is not to say that other information discovered by the asset tracking solution, such as a disk change, added software, or the addition of a new desktop, is not critical to Enterprise Move Add Change. It is just that the items contained in the above table are key to detecting the end-users' movement within the business enterprise. As I said before, it is the end user who either causes or is the recipient of all change associated with the distributed enterprise. It is, therefore, logical that any rational discussion of enterprise change must begin with and be inseparably tied to the end user.

Another aspect of an asset tracking system's Enterprise Move Add Change component is its ability to easily generate both current and historical reports. Predefined "drill-down reports" should be provided as part of the Enterprise Move Add Change component. Such reports provide ready access to the detail underneath the summary information. I will not belabor this point, but it is important to note that all actions resulting from change management involve isolating specifics, both past and present. An effective and accessible report generator can be the difference between success and failure.

Finally, as each organization is unique, it is imperative that both the repository and agents updating the repository be open (accessible) to third-party sources of information and IT systems. See chapter 6.

EMPATHY FOR THE CABLE COMPANY

I began this chapter by criticizing my cable company for failing to recognize that its attempt to improve efficiency was fostering a still greater inefficiency. How easy it is to recognize this flaw in others, but what about us? If we allow the mission-critical distributed enterprise to passively drift on a sea of change, are we any better? The answer is obvious—those who covet success will anchor enterprise changes to the business objectives of the organization.

An Enterprise Move Add Change component, however, is only half of the answer to achieving this objective. The other half is our willingness to look beyond our presuppositions of efficiency and seek the greater benefit of intended purpose. This is sound advice for my cable company and sound advice for those responsible for the IT/business enterprise.

SUMMARY

Change is neither good nor evil, it is simply a breeze that carries us along and with each inhalation brings us one breath closer to death. It is not change that defines our lives, but the destination to which it carries us... this then is our measure, the direction that we allow ourselves to be carried.

CHAPTER 13

HOUSEBOAT

Kay: *(Observing a just-finished sailboat built in her fiancee's basement)* It's beautiful!

Tom (her fiancee): It's taken me more than two and a half years to complete, but it's worth it.

Kay: Why did you decide to build a boat?

Tom: I've always loved the water, loved to work with wood, and I found these award-winning plans for this sloop.

Kay: I mean, why did you decide to build a boat *here*?

Tom: That's a silly question. This is my basement; this is where I have my tools. Where else would I build it?

Kay: No, I mean, how are you going to get it out of here? There's no way that boat is going up those stairs!

Tom: *(Angry)* That's a stupid question! Just leave me alone!

The young woman in this true story is my mother. This exchange happened almost twenty years before I was born, yet my mother never fails to marvel at Tom's miscalculation as she retells the story. Tom had forgotten there are many aspects of technology, whether applied to art, boat building, or distributed enterprise management. Each component of technology must be considered within the context of the mission or you run the risk of facing a very narrow set of stairs with a very wide boat.

Within the context of a mission, technology includes tools (hardware and software), skilled workers, plans/architecture, and logistics. No one of these components has the ability to make the mission successful, but any one of them can scuttle the effort. Mission components and subcomponents are sometimes obscure and sometimes so big that we are unable to focus on them.

This chapter does not attempt to define all of the technologies you must embrace if you are to successfully implement an effective asset tracking system. This would be a fool's errand, as each organization and its enterprise is comprised of a unique set of tools and objectives. Here, I only wish to introduce those items that, if not considered, will prove to be costly detours or even fatal to the mission. As a concession to my editor, I have limited these considerations to a list of eleven "Technology Dos and Don'ts." I have not prioritized these items as their priority will largely depend on the unique circumstances of each organization.

TECHNOLOGY DOS AND DON'TS

DO NOT IMPLEMENT AN ASSET TRACKING SYSTEM THAT IS NOT BUILT ON AN OPEN-DATA STRUCTURE

In the case of an asset tracking system, an ODBC database can be your key to success. The advantages of an ODBC database include:

• It provides you with full access to the repository via SQL query engines.

• It prevents you from becoming locked into a specific vendor for customization and support.

• It allows easy exporting and importing of information from other applications and support tools.

• It provides a robust set of tools to tune and maintain the integrity of the repository.

- It minimizes training and hiring requirements as ODBC-database skills are probably already present within your organization.

DO NOT IMPLEMENT AN ASSET TRACKING SYSTEM THAT
DISTURBS OR CHANGES THE COMMUNICATIONS LINK
BETWEEN YOUR CLIENTS (END-USER WORKSTATIONS)
AND SERVERS

As asset tracking systems, by definition, must "touch" the end-user machines, great care must be taken not to negatively impact the stability of the desktops. One of the most fragile links in the productivity chain is the communications link the desktop has with its server. If a selected asset tracking system requires that special drivers be installed or that parameters of existing communications hardware and/or software on the desktop be changed, a substantial amount of uncertainty is introduced into the network.

Beware! Such changes may appear to be harmless in the lab, but when introduced in the field, they may introduce variables that create conflicts with other mission-critical applications. Arithmetic speaks volumes on this topic. A change in the communications link between the clients and servers that causes intermittent problems with just 15 percent of an enterprise population of 10,000 users, brings forth 1,500 open help desk tickets!

DO SELECT A DESKTOP DISCOVERY PROCESS THAT
IS SELF-DEFINING

Regardless of the asset tracking system selected, some form of discovery (i.e., ascertaining what items make up the desktop) must take place on the desktop. This discovery process is then used to update the repository and provide the capabilities described in earlier chapters. However, what if the link to the repository is down? What if the end users have an immediate need to know configuration information about their desktops, and they do not have access to the repository? What if the users are not connected to the enterprise and wish to convey the status/configuration of their machine to those supporting them? If the selected asset tracking solution has a self-defining discovery process, users can print out or display information about their desktops in a readable/self-defining format (e.g., CPU Type = Pentium, Operating System = Windows NT, etc.).

This capability may rarely be needed, but having it can make the difference in solving a problem in minutes versus days. In addition, it empowers end users to make more intelligent decisions when considering or dealing with self-installed shrink-wrapped applications.

DO NOT SELECT AN ASSET TRACKING SYSTEM THAT IS NOT SCALABLE

Asset tracking is an evolving science. Just two years ago, tracking WWW activity was not considered fundamental to effective enterprise management. Today, any tracking solution that does not address WWW activity is less than state of the art.

It is impossible to predict what hooks and extensions will be required of an enterprise asset tracking system over the next five years; but it is certain that whatever the future holds, it will require more input/output (I/O) and processing capacity. Therefore, whatever asset tracking system is selected, it should run on a wide array of processing platforms, allowing for infinite expansion in the number of supported desktops and servers (remember mergers and acquisitions), and limitless expansion of the information it tracks and stores.

DO CHOOSE A SYSTEM THAT SUPPORTS A WIDE RANGE OF
PLATFORMS AND OPERATING SYSTEMS

Typically, organizations view themselves as having standardized on a desktop platform, yet when I probe deeper, the conversation more typically goes as follows:

Me: What do your desktops look like?

IT Executive: We've standardized on Windows 98.

Me: Then 100 percent of your users are Windows 98?

IT Executive: Well, about 5 to 6 percent are Macintosh, mostly in marketing and senior management.

Me: Any UNIX or DOS desktops floating around?

IT Executive: About 8 percent of the desktops are UNIX, primarily the financial analysts and engineers. And the product providers who run a DOS-based application are around 11 to 12 percent of the population.

Me: So about 75 percent of your users are Windows 98?

IT Executive: Yeah, either Windows 98 now or they're scheduled to be upgraded from Windows 95 to Windows 98.

This composite conversation highlights two truths about most organizations. First, although they have a strong preference for a specific platform, it never really becomes an "enterprise standard." And second, those that fall outside the standard are often the most high-profile users. In the above example, if I had rephrased my question—So how do you feel about an asset tracking solution that excludes a large portion of your senior managers, financial analysts, product providers, and a bunch of people in your marketing department?—I suspect broad-platform support would receive serious consideration.

Even if you have an absolute standard for your enterprise, broad-platform support should still be given serious consideration. Remember that your need for it is as close as the next merger or acquisition.

DO NOT SELECT AN ARCHITECTURE THAT REQUIRES CONSOLIDATION OR RECONCILIATION OF MULTIPLE REPOSITORIES

With the proliferation of client/server applications, the distribution of information across the enterprise has become fashionable. Many applications lend themselves to this physical distribution of data, but asset tracking is not one of them. The true beauty of an enterprise-wide asset tracking solution is its ability to present an accurate model of your enterprise at any level. It provides immediate answers to questions like: Who else has this problem configuration? How do the desktops in the sales department compare to the rest of the corporation? Who is generating the most Internet-initiated traffic? The answers to these questions are available because there is a single central repository of asset information.

Beware of server-based asset tracking systems that require additional steps to generate an enterprise-wide view of your distributed IT assets. Such consolidations can be complex, time- and network-consuming, and are prone to error. In addition, because of these complexities, organizations tend to lessen the frequency of consolidations and thus decrease the utility of the tracking system.

DO SELECT A SYSTEM WITH AN EXTENDABLE ARCHITECTURE

Within this context, extendable pertains to both what is discovered and what is maintained in the repository. Specific questions that should be addressed when considering the "extendability" of the architecture include:

- When a new desktop or server is discovered, what steps, if any, need to be taken to make the appropriate entry into the repository? The repository should automatically create a new record.

- When a new component is discovered on the desktop or server, what steps, if any, need to be taken to make the appropriate entry into the repository? The repository should automatically append the appropriate desktop record.

- What steps, if any, are required to expand the discovery process to include a new device (e.g., credit card reader)? A well-documented software development kit (SDK) should be available to allow organizations to create their own discovery agents.

- Once a new discovery agent is created, what steps are required to populate the desktops and servers with the new agent? The repository should have the ability to automatically populate the enterprise with the new agent.

- Does the proposed system support interactive discovery agents (i.e., agents that query the end user and/or server administrator for information)? If so, are these agents created via the standard SDK? Can interactive agents be defeated by the end user?

DO NOT SELECT AN ASSET TRACKING SOLUTION
WITHOUT INVESTIGATING THE RANGE AND DEPTH OF
THE DISCOVERY PROCESS

Considerations include: What software, hardware components, and communications links can be identified? What operating system configuration information is discovered and tracked? Remember that each of the above questions must be asked for each client and server platform.

DO SELECT A SYSTEM THAT ALLOWS YOU TO BUILD A HISTORICAL RECORD (MULTIPLE SNAPSHOTS) OF EACH DISTRIBUTED ASSET

Questions in this area include:

• How many historical snapshots is the system capable of tracking? The amount of historical information should be limited only by the physical storage capacity of the repository machine.

• How often can snapshots be taken? There should be no limit as to how often a desktop can be inventoried. If the discovery process is transparent to the end-user and server administrators, you should consider collecting two to four snapshots each month. Note: Individual circumstances may dictate a more or less frequent schedule.

• How many desktop, network, and repository resources are required to take a snapshot of the enterprise?

• How are snapshots scheduled? Do all desktops and servers need to be on an identical schedule? You should be able to set schedules in a manner that distributes and optimizes network load.

• What steps must the end user execute to facilitate a snapshot of the desktop? Ideally, no end-user or server-administrator involvement is required.

DO NOT IGNORE THE COMPLEXITY OF IMPLEMENTING AND SUPPORTING THE PROPOSED SYSTEM

Questions that should be addressed include:

• What automated functions are available to initially populate the enterprise desktops with the proposed system? The desktops should be populated via their attached server.

• Can new desktops automatically be populated without involving the end user or support staff? Once the servers are populated, the desktop should be populated the first time it connects into the enterprise.

- When a user accidentally or intentionally removes the tracking application from the desktop, what steps are required to reinstall the application? The software should automatically reinstall the next time the workstation connects to the network.

- What steps are required to implement the system on the enterprise servers? The server should have a point-and-click installation program that requires only the identification of the repository address.

- What skill sets are required to install and maintain the asset repository? Ideally, the repository should come fully populated with functionality and should require no custom programming or consulting. Heavy consulting-based solutions should be avoided as planning and design efforts require significant involvement from your IT staff. In addition, consulting-based solutions take longer to implement, introduce unproven concepts and codes into the solution, typically provide less functionality, and are more expensive. A properly designed asset tracking solution should require no specialized skills other than a technician capable of installing an ODBC database.

DO FOCUS ON UTILITY WHEN SELECTING AN ASSET TRACKING SYSTEM

Often when evaluating technology, we become so engrossed in the metrics of technology that we lose sight of functionality. Consider the following points when evaluating an asset tracking system:

- How broad a spectrum of users will be able to leverage the proposed system? Does the proposed system provide multiple levels of access for different types of users?

- How broad is the utility offered by the proposed solution? Does it only appeal to IT professionals or does it offer specific utility to a range of professionals (e.g., finance, purchasing, help desk, security, etc.)?

- How approachable is the proposed system (easy to use)? Regardless of utility, if it has a daunting interface, it is unlikely that nontechnical users will avail themselves of the potential benefits of an asset tracking system.

- How lucid are the results produced by the proposed system? Any system (even if it's easy to use) that produces confusing or cumbersome results will only be used by the most knowledgeable individuals.

- How much training is required to make a typical user productive? If the proposed system requires formal training before delivering recognizable benefits, it is unlikely that the system will be broadly adopted by the organization's business functions (nontechnical staff and managers). Ideally, formal training can be avoided by selecting a system that has an inviting, intuitive, and familiar interface.

SUMMARY

The primary product of technology is not results or progress or efficiency, but something much greater...opportunity.

CHAPTER 14

LICENSE AND REGISTRATION, PLEASE

AN EVALUATION PARADIGM

Officer: May I see your license and registration, please?

Me: Yes, sir.

Officer: Mr. Jesse, did you know that you were speeding?

Me: Yes, sir.

Officer: Any idea how fast you were going?

Me: No, sir.

Officer: You were doing 52 in a 35 mph zone. You running late?

Me: No.

Officer: Going somewhere special?

Me: Nowhere really, just going for a ride.

Officer: Well, Mr. Jesse, I appreciate your honesty, but I'm going to have to write you up. I'm afraid you're going to be a little late to nowhere, and when you get there you will be $60 lighter.

This incident, upon reflection, taught me one of the great lessons of my adult life: that time, money, and objectives are part of a balanced equation. In this case, I bought time for $60 with no reason or plan as to how to spend it and I got a bonus—two points on my license. As I discovered later in life, time also has the ability to unbalance the equation. In this case, the money and objectives are the given, but time prevents the actuation of a positive result.

I have saved this discussion for the last chapter as it highlights a problem facing you or anyone else who is empowered with the knowledge and desire to implement an effective asset tracking solution. You know what you want and are more than willing to pay the price, and yet the starting gun is silent. Here, time never becomes part of the equation, and the positive result is delayed or never realized.

In considering the concepts outlined in this book, including the compelling return-on-investment (ROI) case, why would any rational manager postpone implementing an asset tracking solution? The answer to this question has more to do with how decisions are made than the decision itself. We have created a decision process for enterprise-based products and solutions that takes a year or more to complete. It involves consultants, industry analysts, and committees, with special consideration being given to strategic vendors, reports, comparative studies, requests for proposals (RFPs), price negotiations, and trials. The result is a confusing array of technically based decision criteria that defy translation into a business case.

I am not dismissing the value of this evaluation cycle, as it was forged around years of experience and is designed to avoid failure. In the case of an asset tracking solution, however, risk aversion is not the primary aim. As we have seen in this text, the opportunity base available through implementing an asset tracking solution is so vast that even a partially effective solution has the ability to produce an extraordinary ROI. Asset tracking does not fit the traditional evaluation model of "precise implementation for marginal returns." Consequently, waiting a year or more to implement a solution is both financially and competitively unsound.

I would not be so bold as to tell you how to redesign your organization's decision process, as it is highly dependent on a myriad of factors. However, I am suggesting the following paradigm when you evaluate an asset tracking solution. Here speed replaces caution in the decision process, as the overwhelming benefits of rapid deployment vastly outweigh the advantages of a tedious investigation.

WEEK 1

Conduct an informal (e.g., "back-of-the-envelope") analysis of potential savings (see chapter 7). Use conservative but realistic estimates and include all areas of potential savings. This should produce a ROI case that will allow you to garner the necessary support for the next step.

WEEKS 1 & 2

Prepare a business case that involves and spans a broad base of functions (e.g., finance, IT, operations, purchasing, help desk, etc.). In doing so, you build a broad base of justification and internal support so if one area fails to meet expectations, other areas will continue to justify the decision. Ways to build such a consensus include: introducing targeted individuals to the case studies and types of analyses covered in this text, arranging for some form of self-directed (e.g., video, CD-ROM, or DVD-ROM) product demonstration, or providing each of them with a copy of this book.

WEEK 2

Verify your business case and "back-of-the-envelope" assumptions with the supporters in each of the functional groups and make appropriate adjustments if necessary.

WEEKS 2 & 3

Solicit a list of "best-of-breed" solutions from a reputable industry analyst.

Weeks 3 & 4

Contact the top three vendors on the above list and compare the various offerings against a matrix of desired features (see chapters 5 and 13). *Note: I have developed a detailed evaluation document for this purpose, but space considerations prohibit me from including it in this text. To order a copy, see page 207.*

Weeks 4 & 5

View a live demonstration (at a customer site) of the top one or two contenders.

Weeks 6 & 7

Select a solution and implement a multiserver, 250-desktop pilot. This should require minimal funding and avoid any extended sign-off cycles. Note: By having this pilot and gathering snapshots twice a day for a two-week period, you can simulate several quarters of activity over a short period of time.

Week 8

Assuming a successful pilot, seek funding for a departmental implementation and begin enterprise implementation. Note: This schedule assumes that the negotiation of the contract and pricing terms, as well as departmental funding efforts, overlap the product evaluations in weeks five, six, and seven.

This eight-week investigation to implement an asset tracking solution may at first sound radical, but it is far less extreme than letting your current base of IT assets go unmanaged for another year. Forward-thinking organizations—perhaps your competitors—are moving quickly in an effort to realize the productivity gains associated with the proactive management of their distributed IT enterprises. Perhaps the most radical concept of all is knowingly to let your competitors have a ten-month lead in such an undertaking.

And what if you discover seven weeks into the eight-week program that you should have selected an alternative product? The answer is to abandon your effort on the first product and install the second. Upon completion of the second eight-week program (implementation of the second solution) you will still only have fifteen weeks invested in implementing a successful solution. And besides, as a highly esteemed CIO once told me, "I'm not sure you have any better chance of picking a winner in twelve months than you do in eight weeks."

I opened this chapter talking about the time-money-objective equation. There is actually a fourth part to that formula—risk. Moving boldly to seize the opportunity of dramatic productivity gains requires that risks be taken. But, oh, how small they seem when compared to the prize. To be certain, there is always a hazard in moving forward, but I encourage you to embrace the chance. For you and Dorothy, in your enterprise and in Oz, shall never find your way home by standing still.

ADDITIONAL INFORMATION

Other documents I have written on this topic include:

- Enterprise Change Worksheet - assists the reader in constructing the costs associated with various enterprise changes.

- Evaluation Checklist - provides a summary of essential asset discovery elements.

- Asset Tracking Features Matrix - summarizes key asset tracking features that should be considered during a product evaluation.

Although these documents do not fit the format of this book, I do make them available free of charge to the reader. If you have an interest in receiving a copy of these documents, simply drop me an e-mail (chrisj@tangram.com) and include the ISBN number on the back cover of the book. Depending on my assistant's schedule, such requests are generally turned around in two to ten days.

INDEX